Right Idea, Right Time

The Fight for Pensacola's Maritime Park

By
Rick Outzen

Prologue

The transformation of Pensacola's waterfront from an industrial wasteland to a vibrant community centerpiece wasn't just about building a park—it was a pivotal battle for our city's future. This book chronicles the struggle to pass the 2006 Community Maritime Park referendum, a campaign that drastically altered Pensacola's trajectory and challenged decades of economic stagnation and resistance to change.

When visitors now stroll along Palafox Street in downtown Pensacola, they experience a thriving city proud of its rich history. They enjoy baseball games at Blue Wahoos Stadium, attend concerts at the Randall K. and Martha A. Hunter Amphitheater, and marvel at one of Florida's most beautiful waterfront settings. Few realize the intense conflict that made this renaissance possible—a referendum fight that divided neighbors, tested friendships, and ultimately redefined how Pensacolians view their community and its potential.

The story of the referendum has been told before, but memories fade, and emotions create different impressions of what truly happened. Over the past year, I have interviewed dozens of people who were directly involved in the campaign, examined archives from the Pensacola News Journal and Inweekly, and unearthed posts from my blog. For each person I interviewed, many others could have offered their perspectives, but at some point, the writing had to begin.

This book aims to provide the definitive account of how a small group of visionaries overcame entrenched opposition to create lasting change. It examines how their proposal for a maritime museum, conference center, and ballpark became the catalyst that would transform not just our waterfront but our community's self-image. More importantly, it documents how this fight empowered a new generation of leaders and proved that Pensacola could dream bigger.

The Community Maritime Park referendum represented a crucial turning point between those who saw Pensacola's potential and those who feared change. Some participants were more honest than others as the debate raged over nearly two years, but the battle transcended a simple question about a ballpark. It marked a watershed moment when Pensacola finally chose progress over paralysis.

As you read this account, you'll witness how dedicated individuals found unexpected courage in the face of personal attacks, how lifelong residents discovered new determination to improve their hometown, and how a struggling newspaper found its voice. In these pages, I hope you'll not only learn what really happened but also appreciate how one project can profoundly change a city's destiny.

Rick Outzen

Table of Contents

Prologue i

Chapter 1: Waffle House 1

Chapter 2: The Comeback Kid.................................. 6

Chapter 3: Unlikely Companions...............................11

Chapter 4: Not A City Plan...................................... 18

Chapter 5: Recruiting The Admiral 27

Chapter 6: A Ballpark Needed 34

Chapter 7: Preparing for the City Council 44

Chapter 8: Setting a New Course 52

Chapter 9: Opportunity of a Lifetime..................... 61

Chapter 10: The Gindroz Touch.............................. 66

Chapter 11: Dollars & Cents 76

Chapter 12: A Long Hot Summer 83

Chapter 13: The Opposition Solidifies................... 92

Chapter 14: Hammering Out Details....................... 98

Chapter 15: Dollars Get Tighter...108

Chapter 16: Prelude to the Vote 116

Chapter 17: The Council Vote..123

Chapter 18: Sides Chosen 134

Chapter 19: Save Our City 143

Chapter 20: Another Loss 150

Chapter 21: A Blog is Born 160

Chapter 22: Smoking Gun 169

Chapter 23: Trading Punches 175

Chapter 24: For the Kids..186

Chapter 25: Momentum Shifts..198

Chapter 26: The Home Stretch 211

Chapter 27: Last Ditch Efforts 227

Chapter 28: The Vote 237

Epilogue: 247

Chapter 1:
Waffle House

September 2006

Late on a hot, humid September night, I hunched over my black coffee in a Waffle House on the edge of downtown Pensacola, listening to my friends' conversation. We had the whole place to ourselves. Out of the corner of my eye, I watched the fry cook methodically cleaning his grill while the lone waitress dragged a rag across the countertops.

My companions were both "Friends of Bill." As the youngest of our trio, I clung to Hemingway's mantra: "Write drunk, edit sober." My coffee choice betrayed my reality—a long night of editing still awaited me back at the office. The pair in recovery had very successful businesses while I struggled to pay bills and cover payroll.

Go figure.

While supporters had gathered to mark our improbable political triumph in Pensacola's historic Seville Quarter, amid brick archways and gas-lit corridors, our small group had slipped away from the main celebration, seeking a quiet corner to process the day's events. As steam rose from our coffee mugs, conversation turned to the two visionaries who hadn't lived to see this moment. We clinked our cups together in their memory.

In the wake of Hurricane Ivan's devastating strike on the Florida Panhandle in 2004, Pensacola, a modest city of under 55,000 residents, was desperate for any triumph. The Category 3 hurricane slammed into the Gulf Coast with 120-mph winds and a 15-foot storm surge that devastated coastal communities. Buildings that had stood for over a century were reduced to rubble overnight. The storm had left an indelible mark on the region, claiming eight lives across Escambia and Santa Rosa counties while forcing thousands to evacuate.

As Ivan carved its path northward through Alabama, North Carolina, and ultimately New York, it inflicted more than seven billion dollars in damage. The impact on Northwest Florida was particularly severe—FEMA documented over 3,700 families rendered homeless. Meanwhile, the U.S. Army Corps of Engineers launched a massive operation to install temporary blue plastic sheeting (which locals grimly called "blue roofs") on more than 51,000 damaged structures.

Downtown Pensacola had been submerged under several feet of saltwater, destroying businesses and crippling infrastructure. Power outages lasted for weeks in some areas. The city's historic district suffered catastrophic damage, with century-old oak trees uprooted and iconic buildings severely compromised. Nearly every resident had a personal story of loss—whether a home, a business, or cherished possessions.

Before the hurricane struck, the region was already struggling economically. A 2001 analysis by the Pensacola News Journal highlighted a troubling wage gap: workers in Escambia and Santa Rosa counties earned an average of one dollar less per hour compared to the state average—a stark reversal from twenty years prior, when local wages exceeded the Florida average by fifty cents.

This decline stemmed from a dramatic shift in the local economy. The manufacturing sector, once comprising 15 percent of employment, had dwindled to just 5 percent, with workers forced into lower-paying service industry jobs. The Naval Air Station, a traditional source of well-compensated civilian positions with substantial benefits, shed over 3,500 jobs between 1990 and 2000.

Meanwhile, economic vitality migrated eastward along the Panhandle. Pensacola's per capita income lagged behind both Fort Walton Beach and Panama City. The transformation of St. Joe Paper Company—Florida's second-largest private landowner—into the St. Joe Company symbolized this shift. Their upscale developments in Walton and Bay counties attracted affluent buyers from major Southern cities like Atlanta, Birmingham, and Nashville.

Pensacola faced challenges that went beyond economic hardship—its very identity was shaken to the core. As the seat of Escambia County, it witnessed one of Florida's most egregious corruption scandals. The situation reached a breaking point in 2002 when Governor Jeb Bush had to take the extraordinary step of removing four out of five county commissioners, who faced charges ranging from violations of open government laws to accepting bribes.

This political turmoil reignited interest in establishing a charter government, essentially a local constitution that would give the county more control over its governmental structure rather than following the state-mandated five-commissioner system. Despite Escambia being among the few counties of its size without a charter, repeated attempts to change this proved unsuccessful.

The community had narrowly rejected charter government three times before, with the 1995 attempt falling short by just fifty-six votes. However, the 2004 referendum marked a stark turning point. It failed by over 10,000 votes, the largest margin of defeat yet. This overwhelming rejection suggested a deeper crisis: Escambia County's residents had become profoundly disillusioned with their local government.

The Waffle House waitress swept past with fresh coffee, topping off our mugs before gliding over to a young family huddled near the window facing the Pensacola Civic Center. My companions, Quint Studer and Mort O'Sullivan, remained lost in conversation, savoring the evening's triumph as steam curled up from their cups. The clinking of ceramic and the gentle murmur of late-night patrons drifting in created a cocoon around our shared memories of the path that led us here.

Chapter 2:
The Comeback Kid

Pensacola tended to reject outsiders for much of its history. The city feasted on those born north of the Mason-Dixon line with their bright ideas, and who especially spouted about Pensacola's potential. Pensacolians relished taking their money and watching the Northerners disappear as their plans fell apart. They thought Quint Studer would be another notch in their belts, but they misjudged him.

In 1996, Baptist Health Care sought a transformative leader for its Pensacola facility. They found their answer in a hospital administrator from Chicago who had achieved remarkable results as chief operating officer of Holy Cross Hospital, improving patient satisfaction from three to 73 percent in just six months. This accomplishment had earned Holy Cross the coveted "Comeback of the Year" award from Hospitals & Health Networks & American Hospital Association.

Fred Donovan served as chairman of the Baptist Health Care System board and CEO of Baskerville Donovan, a local engineering firm. He reflected on their decision decades later: "We knew we had to do something about that. Who's number one in the nation? It was Holy Cross, and this guy, Quint Studer, was running it. We brought him down a couple of times. And then, finally, we hired him and made him the president of Baptist Hospital."

What set Studer apart was his unconventional approach to leadership. Rather than claiming a prestigious corner office in Baptist Tower's C-Suite, he chose a basement location next to the cafeteria. Donovan observed, "He had plate glass windows so employees could see inside his work area. When they walked by, he would tap on the window, bring them in, and ask what he could do to make the hospital better. They made recommendations, and Quint would make it happen."

The results were impressive: patient satisfaction soared to 99 percent, employee turnover dropped to 12 percent, and the hospital added $1.8 million to its bottom line. Awards followed, including the Voluntary Hospital Association Leadership Award, the Modern Healthcare Sodexo Marriott Service Excellence Award, and the USA Today Quality Cup. Studer became the only healthcare professional to be named a "Master of Business" by Inc. Magazine.

In 2000, Studer leveraged his success to launch Studer Group, a healthcare consulting firm that grew to over a hundred employees by 2004. But his path to success wasn't always smooth.

Growing up in LaGrange, Illinois, he faced numerous challenges. He slept in a converted walk-in closet in his family's modest two-bedroom house. Living with a hearing impairment in one ear and partial hearing in the other, he developed a speech impediment that made school particularly challenging.

"I perfected how to hide behind whoever was sitting in front of me," he shared.

Despite academic struggles, a surprising ACT score opened doors to the University of Wisconsin-Whitewater. His career began in special education, but personal demons emerged.

Describing his battle with alcoholism, he said, "When I drank, I felt confident. I could talk to people and not be afraid, but it destroyed every relationship I had. On Christmas Day, 1982, I hit rock bottom. I was hungover from drinking until the bars closed on Christmas Eve, and sitting in my living room staring at a Christmas tree without any presents. I was 31, with two failed marriages and deep in debt. Something had to change."

His recovery journey eventually landed him at Holy Cross Hospital in Chicago. The struggling facility presented enormous challenges. Vendors delivered supplies only if there was a check at the loading dock. If the new management team failed to turn things around, the hospital would close or be sold.

All of Quint's old fears of failure began to resurface. After about two months, he wanted to quit. However, the new Holy Cross CEO, Mark Clement, wasn't about to give up. The management team held an off-site retreat to set new goals for the upcoming year. The team decided that Holy Cross should raise its reported 3 percent patient satisfaction to 75 percent in one year.

Reflecting on his early days there, Quint recalled, "I was chosen to work on patient satisfaction by default. The finance guy took the financial goals. HR had the ones involving employees. The chief nurse took quality, and I was left with patient satisfaction."

Seeking guidance, he reached out to Press Ganey, which told him no hospital had ever achieved such dramatic improvement in patient satisfaction. Looking beyond healthcare, he found inspiration from Southwest Airlines, which had started flights from Chicago's Midway Airport and had received national accolades for its customer service. Its leaders advised: "Focus on the employees, not the patients."

Quint's approach evolved: "We started putting copy machines near the workstations so they wouldn't have to leave their floor to make copies. We opened the cafeteria at night so the late shifts could eat. We got them more IV poles. It really was pretty minor things once we started listening."

Patient satisfaction ratings began shooting up each month. "The more we worked with the employees, the happier our patients became. The next year, we jumped to the 94th percentile, and the hospital made money."

This success caught Baptist Hospital's attention, leading to his move to Pensacola. Naysayers knew very little about Quint's background and saw him as just another wealthy outsider whom they could run off. However, his experiences had prepared him well. His past struggles with rejection and failure had forged a resilient leader ready to make a lasting impact on the community.

Chapter 3:
Unlikely Companions

In the Waffle House booth, Quint nursed his coffee alongside an odd pair—the polished community leader who moved effortlessly through Pensacola's corridors of power and me, the agitator whose questions and criticisms had earned me a reputation as a thorn in the establishment's side.

Mort O'Sullivan III was Quint's trusted financial adviser and one of his closest friends in Pensacola. He led Northwest Florida's largest CPA firm, O'Sullivan Creel. He was in line to be the next board chair of the Pensacola Chamber of Commerce.

Unlike many of his peers who boasted five-generation ties to Pensacola, O'Sullivan earned his position as one of the most respected Baby Boomers. He gained influence in Pensacola as the World War II-era leaders began to fade, becoming the most diplomatic and least controversial of the city's power brokers.

Mort's grandfather, John Mort O'Sullivan, was part of the wave of World War II veterans who sought their fortune in Pensacola after the war. The New Yorker had worked for General Motors for 22 years, handling sales promotions and public relations throughout the southeastern United States. In 1944, he enlisted and served in the Army at the Pentagon. When the war ended, he returned to GM and traveled Central America for three years, assisting GM agencies.

In 1948, he opened Mort O'Sullivan Pontiac at 132 East Gregory Street, less than two blocks from the Waffle House where we drank coffee. Mort's father, J. Mort O'Sullivan Jr., practiced law in the Pensacola area, serving for a time as the Gulf Breeze city judge before dying suddenly at age 49.

Mort graduated from Pensacola Catholic High in 1969. Steve Romero, his best friend since fifth grade at St. Stephen's Catholic School, quarterbacked the Crusaders, while Mort played wide receiver. When Romero received a football scholarship to the University of Florida, Mort wanted to follow him to Gainesville.

"We raised hell together, did all kinds of bad stuff, just had a great time," Mort recalled. He went to see David Levin, the law partner of Reubin Askew, who would be elected governor two years later. Levin had graduated from Pensacola High School at 15, earned a degree in economics from Duke University, and was number two in his law class at the University of Florida.

"I told David I was thinking of maybe going down and walking on at Gainesville," shared Mort, who weighed 155 pounds and stood slightly over six feet as a high school senior. "He looked at me and said, 'What other choices do you have?' I said, 'Well, I have a full academic scholarship to Vanderbilt and WL. And he said, 'You need to turn north because they will kill you down there.'"

Mort continued, "I went to Washington and Lee University, where I spent my time partying and focusing on fraternities and road trips. By the end of my first year, I had a 2.0 GPA and needed to maintain a 3.0 to keep my scholarship. They changed it to half a loan and half a scholarship. At the end of my second year, my cumulative GPA remained at 2.0, and they told me I would be on my own from then on. At that time, the University of West Florida was only three years old, and I realized I needed to go home and enroll at UWF."

He took courses in mathematics, accounting, and anthropology. "I was just a lost kid. In the middle of the semester, I'm starting to do really well in accounting. The chairman, Tom Committe, took me aside and said, 'I've looked at your transcript and test scores. They don't match. You've obviously been a screw-up. I want you to know that everybody who graduated with a degree in accounting here has gotten a job."

Mort had just married his high school sweetheart, Nancy, and soon had a child on the way. He buckled down and earned his bachelor's degree in accounting, graduating magna cum laude. He received six job offers, became a licensed certified public accountant, and began his career with Touche Ross and Company, an international accounting firm in Atlanta.

After his father died in December 1974, he moved back home and went to work for Saltmarsh, Cleaveland and Gund, but soon set up his firm. His first clients were the parents of a high school friend who owned Sunray Hotel on Pensacola Beach and Rita's Dress Shop in the mall.

In 1981, Mort formed O'Sullivan, Patton, and Jacobi. Over the next two decades, he added partners and merged with several firms until he became the managing partner of Florida's eighth-largest CPA firm, O'Sullivan Creel.

His path to becoming a community leader began slowly but grew steadily. "When I was at Saltmarsh, Fred Gund came to me and said there was a vacancy on a board of good citizens. He thought I should consider going and helping out. And here I am, a first-year accountant; I'm thinking this is a little early, but I agreed. It was the Pensacola Heritage Foundation, of which I later became president."

Next, he was asked to be the treasurer of the Girl Scouts. When Lewis Bear, Jr. helped launch Big Brothers Big Sisters, Bear was the first chairman, and Mort was the second. "After that, I found myself getting on boards all the time, including Baptist Health Care, where I served for 21 years."

At Baptist, Mort chaired the finance committee. He first met Quint on a board retreat at Point Clear, a resort on Mobile Bay in nearby Baldwin County, Alabama. "Quint really ruffled feathers. He parked his car in the furthest spot in the parking lot, and he was just some kind of character."

During a break, they discovered that both were in recovery. As Quint began to improve Baptist's patient satisfaction scores, hospitals from across the country flocked to learn how the inner-city hospital achieved this.

"It was Quint, and he started doing speeches in town for free to the community," Mort said. "I attended one of his talks. Quint mentioned that his accounting firm wasn't providing him with good service. It was a holy day of obligation. During lunch, I asked if he wanted to go to Mass with me at St. Michael's. On the way back, we talked about how we could be his accounting firm and scheduled a time for him to meet our team."

He continued, "When he visited the office, I got tied up with a client and left him in our lobby. I finally got free and asked him to go back to my office. Quint said, 'We don't need to talk. I'm bringing my business here because the ten minutes I spent sitting in your lobby with your director of first impressions (the name we put on the receptionist's desk) convinced me that this firm has a culture where I would be happy. And we just started from there."

In 2001, the News Journal asked fifty community members to vote for the area's top twenty leaders, and Mort made the list. In 2002, the Greater Pensacola Chamber awarded him the prestigious Pensacola Area

Commitment to Excellence (PACE) Business Leader of the Year award. The following year, Mort was named to the Florida Chamber's board of directors.

When Mort O'Sullivan spoke, people usually listened. However, the political fight he celebrated over coffee with Quint and me was different.

The Wild Card

I am unsure how to include myself in this story. I publish an alt-weekly in a Southern town that is too small to support our publication. My newspaper had several names over its first seven years: Pensacola Independent, Independent Florida Sun, Independent Sun, and Independent News. Today, we are simply Inweekly.

I had survived a three-year fight for editorial control with Joe Scarborough, a former congressman. The fight finally ended in 2003, when he left Pensacola to pursue a career at MSNBC. My investors abandoned me after Hurricane Ivan, forcing me to use my credit cards to keep the newspaper afloat. I couldn't blame them; they had their issues recovering from the hurricane, and the paper had only just begun to break even after five years.

The Independent News endured because I believed someone had to challenge the status quo if Pensacola would ever progress. I also believed in the power of the press.

I grew up in Greenville, Mississippi—a town known for cotton and its daily newspaper, The Delta Democrat Times. The paper's owner, publisher, and editor, Hodding Carter II, was known for his hard-hitting editorials. He garnered national acclaim for his writing against segregation, White Citizens' Councils, and the Jim Crow laws of his time, earning the title "Spokesman of the New South." He won the Pulitzer Prize in 1946 for his editorials.

People may have disagreed with Big Hodding's editorials, but they read and discussed them daily. I saw the difference a newspaper could make and tried to do the same with the Independent News.

Quint's money and Mort's Pensacola connections were significant to the night's political victory. I drank Waffle House coffee with them because I was the wild card that the opposition never figured out how to handle.

Chapter 4:
Not A City Plan

October 2004

Pensacola Mayor John Fogg and City Manager Tom Bonfield called a meeting with five business leaders to discuss how the city should rebuild after Hurricane Ivan. They met in a small building that Jim Cronley owned behind the offices of Terhaar & Cronley General Contractors.

A former Army helicopter pilot who served during the Vietnam War, Cronley spent three decades building homes, subdivisions, high-rise condominiums, hotels, and commercial buildings throughout the Southeast. He was also a past president of the Home Builders Association of West Florida and was named the Pensacola Chamber's Business Leader of the Year in 1983.

The builder led much of the area's economic development efforts for years. He often used his private plane to visit businesses interested in relocating to Pensacola and fly them here to review sites.

Fogg and Bonfield wanted to meet there because the storm had damaged Pensacola City Hall, and they needed a place away from the media. The previous week, a group had flown to Pensacola from

Homestead, Florida, to meet area leaders at Pensacola Junior College's Hagler Auditorium and share how their South Florida town had recovered from Hurricane Andrew, the worst recorded storm in U.S. history at the time.

Homestead established the "We Will Rebuild" task force, which united public, private, and nonprofit resources to develop a vision for a better community. The vision involved replacing and repairing damaged residences and constructing a $7 million community and youth sports complex.

Former We Will Rebuild executive director Tom David told the Pensacola audience, "Believe it or not, you have an opportunity here to make some positive changes for the long term."

At Cronley's office, Fogg and Bonfield sought input on how to help their hurricane-battered town recover. Mort had a seat at the table.

"We started talking about what we can do as a community," Mort recalled. "It came up that the Homestead leaders had centered their recovery around one significant project—a youth sports complex—to inspire the community."

He suggested the Trillium site on Pensacola Bay, across from Pensacola City Hall, for a ballpark and maritime museum. "I remember two people in a room calling it the worst idea they had ever heard. They wanted condos on the site."

However, Bonfield didn't dismiss the idea. He said, "If that's ever going to happen, the city will not drive it. We just had our hats handed to us on the first Trillium proposal. This must come from somewhere in the community, not City Hall."

Trillium

The Trillium property got its name from a Washington development company, Trillium Corp., which paid $4.6 million for about twenty-eight vacant acres of Pensacola Bay waterfront in 1992. The site had been home to a Chevron USA fuel storage facility for thirty years until it closed in the mid-1980s.

Trillium and the City partnered on a master land use plan for the last large chunk of open property downtown. Bullock Tice Associates managed the design team that Trillium hired to explore the possibility of creating a festival marketplace featuring shops, homes, a hotel, and dockside facilities for a cruise stop. The city asked its Community Redevelopment Agency (CRA) director, Jennifer Fleming, and planner Cyril Paumier of LDR International to study the feasibility of the proposed development.

In April 1995, planners unveiled the Pensacola Waterfront Redevelopment Plan. Based on input from a series of public workshops, the plan focused on increasing public access to Pensacola Bay, creating more public spaces, improving walkability, and developing attractions for locals and tourists.

For centuries, the waterfront had been principally used for shipping and commercial fishing, with few public areas, except for the Bayfront Auditorium at the end of Palafox Street. The plan called for continuous public access and amenity corridors along Bayfront Parkway, Main Street, and Cedar Street. People-friendly pedestrian spaces would link downtown to the waterfront.

The redevelopment plan embraced the development of the Bayfront Auditorium into a regional Bay attraction headquarters, with an adjacent marina becoming a water transportation hub. The Port of Pensacola would remain, but adjoining land would be considered for redevelopment.

Trillium offered three alternative concepts for its site. Alternative One featured a marina urban village and waterfront hotel as its anchors, with a full-service marina on the adjacent, city-owned Bruce Beach property. Alternative Two included a hotel, conference center, and cruise boat operations as the primary uses of the Trillium property. Alternative Three proposed an institutional campus development.

The Trillium redevelopment never happened. While city leaders debated the alternatives for months, company officials decided the site was too far from their headquarters to develop adequately. Trillium would sell its Pensacola properties and withdraw from the area. Some blamed the developer's decision on the failure of a state referendum that would have authorized a limited number of casinos in eight counties, including Escambia.

The city faced another issue: the aging Bayfront Auditorium needed to be replaced. Opened at the end of South Palafox Street overlooking Pensacola Bay in 1955, the facility served as the city's largest music venue for decades. Elvis Presley, Patsy Cline, and Jerry Lee Lewis performed on its stage, as did the Bee Gees, Bob Dylan, No Doubt, and Green Day. When Escambia County opened the Pensacola Civic Center in the mid-eighties, musical acts began to perform at the larger venue, the auditorium's revenue dwindled, and the city facility's losses started to mount.

Even though Trillium didn't follow through with its projects, the 2005 plan became a guide for waterfront redevelopment. The CRA tackled some of the plan's proposed projects, including sidewalks along Bayfront Park, a marina on South Palafox, additional public parking, and the completion of Port Royal Phase II, a gated community east of the Trillium site that Cronley had developed in the 1980s.

In November 1998, Tom Bonfield began working as Pensacola's new city manager. Bonfield had been the city manager of Temple Terrace, a Tampa suburb of about 22,000 people, since 1985. He aimed to revitalize Pensacola's downtown. With a new century approaching,

Bonfield proposed demolishing the aging Bayfront Auditorium and possibly purchasing the Trillium site for festivals.

"Beginning last spring, it became obvious to me that the city did not have an overall strategy for this area," the city manager told the daily newspaper. "With this strategy, we're not just drawing pretty pictures of facilities, but doing something that could spur private development."

The Pensacola City Council approved his recommendation to rehire LDR International to review and update the 1995 plan, understanding that the city planned to purchase the Trillium site and had allocated Local Option Sales Tax funds for a waterfront festival park, a new Bayfront Auditorium, and new downtown parking facilities.

The city leaders appointed four dozen community leaders and residents to a Waterfront Development Strategic Advisory Committee to collaborate with the firm. The committee held four public workshops over six months. Meanwhile, the city purchased the Trillium property for $3.45 million in May 2000.

The advisory committee delivered the Pensacola Waterfront Development Plan 2000 to the City Council in late 2000. The plan described the Trillium site as the largest vacant parcel on the waterfront and having the greatest potential for mixed uses. The site could accommodate a new auditorium, 142,000 square feet of mixed-use space, and 969 surface parking spaces. Over half of the site would be open space, including ten acres for a public park and five to six acres of shoreline and boulevard space.

In March 2001, the City Council hired Bullock Tice to design a master plan based on the new waterfront plan. The final design of the Waterfront Festival Park accommodated large festivals and special events and included an auditorium with a capacity of 3,000 people. The estimated cost of the project was $40 million.

However, the business community questioned the design. The Pensacola Chamber's Progress 2005 Committee, which included Mort and several top leaders on the News Journal's 2001 list, asked the Pensacola City Council to reconsider the master plan. The committe worried about how the project's cost increased from its original $15 million estimate to $40 million. It disagreed with using all the property for public and municipal purposes and missing the opportunity for the land to create jobs and boost the city's economy.

The Independent News covered the business community's pushback in May 2002 and interviewed several Progress 2005 Committee members. Architect Brian Spencer said, "If the city embarks on a project of this ambitious economic magnitude, it must be certain it is allocating the taxpayers' money wisely. If the current design is not significantly modified, I predict this publicly funded project will be one of Pensacola's blunders."

Councilman Marty Donovan also objected to the design. On "Pensacola Speaks" on WCOA 1370 AM, he said, "This is an example of runaway government. It has gotten totally out of control for a city of 56,000."

Bonfield defended the plan, citing the nearly three years of public input and workshops. "In my twenty-five years, this by far has been the most deliberate process and the most public participation that I've ever seen."

He added, "This is a huge deal. It's a tremendous opportunity for the city to put a better face on a waterfront that's very industrial and underutilized and make it something that for the next fifty years will make downtown more of a destination in Pensacola."

Mayor Fogg agreed. "The Trillium project will make downtown very vibrant. It'll be something to be very proud of."

When the Pensacola City Council voted to proceed with the waterfront project in November 2002, a newly formed political action committee, Citizens Against Trillium, announced a petition drive to force a referendum on the project. Under the city charter, the group needed to collect 5,550 signatures from registered city voters within sixty days. Since the charter's adoption in 1931, Pensacola had never had a referendum seeking to overturn a council decision.

On January 21, 2003, forty members of Citizens Against Trillium paraded six blocks along Government Street to deliver 8,572 signatures to the city clerk before the noon deadline. After verifying the signatures, the Pensacola City Council approved a mail-in referendum to be held on March 25.

The voters rejected the park, with 62 percent voting against it. Over 19,740 people voted, the largest turnout ever in a single-issue election for a city or county. UWF political science professor Jim Witt warned that the results may have awakened sleeping giants, as voters discovered their power to overturn council votes.

He told the News Journal, "Well, the City Council's going to be goosey all the time. They're not going to know what to do at one time or another."

Witt was correct. Bonfield and Fogg needed to take a different approach in October 2004. If the visionary project to help Pensacola's recovery included a ballpark and a maritime museum built on the Trillium site, Quint and retired Vice Admiral Jack Fetterman would have to buy into and promote the vision.

Chapter 5:
Recruiting The Admiral

November 2004

When Mort left Cronley's, he called Quint, who also owned the Pelicans, an independent minor league baseball team that played its games at the University of West Florida. Mort had been helping him find a site to build a ballpark downtown.

When Quint answered, he said, "We just had an exciting meeting, my friend."

Mort shared the details of the meeting and the proposed visionary project. Quint liked the idea.

The leader pushing for the maritime museum was retired Vice Admiral Jack Fetterman, the president and CEO of the Naval Aviation Museum Foundation. To broach the idea to the admiral, Mort needed the assistance of architect Miller Caldwell, Jr., who aided Fetterman in expanding the Naval Aviation Museum.

The Rockstar

Jack first came to Pensacola in 1955 to attend the Aviation Officer Candidate School aboard NAS Pensacola. He returned as a vice admiral in 1991 to serve as the chief of Naval Education and Training.

He wasn't very tall, but his energy and positivity filled a room. No task was too difficult for Jack.

"Everywhere we've been, he was a rockstar," his widow Nancy shared. "He led a blessed life and was a kind, good person. He agonized over having to take somebody out of flight training. He would bring them into his office and say, 'You're going to do great things in your life, but this is not one of them.' And they were happy. It was just amazing to me."

Miller worked with Jack on several projects and often received phone calls daily. He said, "Jack was a master motivator who had a unique way of selling a vision, unlike how most other people do. He was very smooth in engaging you, pulling from you what you wanted, and giving you back what he thought you wanted. You would get excited; he would get even more excited, and he'd throw his arms up and say, 'Let's go do it.'"

Before returning to Pensacola, he was the commander of the Naval Air Force, U.S. Pacific Fleet in San Diego. Jack oversaw eight aircraft carriers, eighteen naval air stations, and twenty million miles of the

Pacific Ocean. As his tour of duty ended, he wanted to manage the entire U.S. Pacific Fleet, but they offered him a post in Pensacola since the fleet position wasn't available.

However, his naval career was derailed. A member of his staff was accused of making homosexual advances. Jack sent the complaint to the man's commanding officer, and the sailor was reprimanded and ordered to undergo counseling for alcohol abuse. The Navy later reopened the case, discharged the man, and suspended Jack for failing to refer the case to criminal investigators.

With the Tailhook scandal occurring only two years earlier, Jack did not want to embroil the Navy in another controversy. He denied any wrongdoing but accepted a one-star rank demotion and retired from active duty. Six months later, he appealed the decision, and his rank of three stars was restored, thanks to grassroots efforts from colleagues and friends who viewed the punishment as unjust.

While Jack dealt with the demotion, retired Admiral Maurice Weisner stepped down from the Naval Aviation Museum Foundation after fourteen years as its president. Weisner wanted Jack to succeed him, and he did so in 1993.

Jack and Nancy became very active in the community. Nancy focused on preserving Pensacola's history and took on St. Michael's Cemetery as a project. Jack chaired the Pensacola Chamber of Commerce and the Blue Angel Golf Classic.

Jack also worked vigorously to enhance the National Flight Academy at the National Museum of Naval Aviation. The idea originated with Skip Furlong, the retired rear admiral who served as the foundation's executive vice president. In the early 1990s, Furlong established the academy as a weeklong summer camp where seventh and eighth graders enjoyed activities at the museum and the Naval Air Station.

When he took over the museum, Jack pushed to elevate the Flight Academy to parity with NASA's Marshall Space Flight Center in Huntsville, Alabama. In May 1999, he announced a capital campaign to raise $25 million to add more display space for Navy aircraft and to build a facility for the flight academy, which he referred to as the museum's "next evolution."

Middle and high school students would sleep, eat, and learn in a simulated aircraft carrier environment. They would be given flight suits and divided into squadrons. The curriculum would inspire them in math, science, and technology. The retired admiral envisioned children from around the country attending the academy and offering scholarships for those who couldn't afford the tuition.

Miller got involved in the design because the New York firm hired to do the work needed local representation. However, the initial construction estimates were nearly $65 million.

Jack called the architect and said, "I don't know if we can raise that kind of money. This just isn't going to make it; it's going to die."

He assured the admiral that he would find a way to make the expansion happen. "A lot of the problem is that when you take an old building and add a new wing, all the new building codes must apply to both structures."

The architect separated the new hangar and the flight academy from the original museum to create a museum campus. Miller said, "We put the new hangar adjacent to the other hangars, and then we created the Flight Academy for kids, and we did it within the money that Jack had."

He added, "Then, Jack said, 'Man, you saved my ass. Now you're going to help me save this maritime museum."

The Maritime Museum

Nancy recalled, "Jack was quietly magnetic and could talk anyone into anything. He wanted to find a certain aircraft that had crashed into Pensacola and convince the Navy to use its radar to locate it. After they did, he contacted Dr. Judy Bense, who ran the UWF archaeology program. From that point, Jack became very interested in marine archaeology and thought it would perfectly complement a maritime museum."

Jack envisioned a museum celebrating Pensacola's colonial history, shipbuilding, commercial fishing, and role in naval aviation.

"He didn't have anybody willing to help him," Miller said. "He came to my office and started sharing his ideas."

The architect asked Jack why he wanted to drag people downtown while trying to grow the naval museum.

"Well, have you ever thought about the fact that when people come here, they won't come back unless there are more things for them to do?" he replied. "The maritime museum is a natural fit. It'll synergize both downtown and the Naval Aviation Museum. It'll energize the beach and the entire area."

Miller said, "He was a big thinker, yet he was able to assemble an army to help him get things done. I got excited and agreed to help, and we began trying to define what it was he wanted to build."

They researched other naval museums around the world. The more they learned, the more excited Jack became.

"Jack said this could be really something big, and he told me to go through and evaluate what the City has to offer us on the port and over at the Trillion property, and let's see what we can do," Miller said. "We took two proposals, one for each site. We talked to Bonfield, and he was somewhat cold on the maritime museum, probably because of the Trillium fight."

However, the idea began to win supporters after the Trillium referendum failed. The UWF Haas Center for Business Research and

Economic Development estimated that its spending impact would be between $25 million and $57 million and would support over 400 jobs.

For weeks in early 2004, the daily newspaper and the community debated whether the Port of Pensacola or the Trillium property would be the best option for the maritime museum. The New Journal's editorial board refused to take a stand: "Whether the museum is built on the Trillium site or the Port of Pensacola, it will celebrate and teach the maritime history of the Pensacola Bay Area, a solid symbol of a community's pride in its heritage and history."

In May 2004, market research commissioned by the city's Port Business Strategy Analysis Committee questioned the Haas Center's estimation of 700,000 visitors annually. The research predicted that the actual traffic would be half of that figure. Meanwhile, the project's budget escalated to $20 million, but community leaders remained confident that Fetterman would raise the money.

While it conceptually approved the maritime museum's placement on the Trillium site, the Pensacola City Council voted to refer the proposal to city staff and the Port Business Strategy Analysis Committee for further review, where it remained in limbo.

Chapter 6:
A Ballpark Needed

December 2004

Quint and his wife, Rishy Studer, purchased the Pensacola Pelicans midway through the 2002 season when the previous owners failed to make payroll. The team was part of the six-team Southeastern League and played its home games at Pensacola Junior College.

The team had a winning record, but attendance averaged fewer than 500 fans per game. The league commissioner couldn't find an owner that the investors would accept. In early July, the commissioner forced the team manager out, even though the Pelicans had the league's best record at 17-10.

The Southeastern League was started by the management group that owned the Montgomery, Alabama Wings. This group needed an owner to fund the team and ensure its continuation. Pensacola baseball fans wondered whether the league would survive its first season.

On July 16, 2002, the league announced Quint Studer as the Pelicans' new owner and former local high school baseball star Pete Della Ratta, the team's all-star pitcher, as the player-manager. At a press conference, Quint promised to turn the team into a first-rate franchise.

He shared that he and Rishy loved the atmosphere when they attended games.

When he discovered Pelican's ownership was available, he asked Mort about the investment. He joked that Mort replied, "Quint, if you want to lose some money, this might be how to do it."

The Studers bought the franchise for $93,000—$17,500 for the team and $75,500 to cover the team's estimated losses for the season. They wouldn't take a salary or reimburse themselves. Quint said, "We're doing this for the community. It's a way to give back."

The new owner had a rude awakening before his team played its first home game under his ownership. The Montgomery Wings management called and said their players refused to play because they hadn't been paid. Quint was stuck because he had already paid for a fireworks show to celebrate the Pelicans' second opening night. He agreed to cover the Wings' travel, hotel, and meals to make the game happen.

The Pelicans won the league championship, defeating Montgomery in front of 700 fans at Pensacola Junior College. By the end of the season, the Southeastern League had dropped to four teams.

In 2003, the Studers hired former Cincinnati Reds outfielder Bernie Carbo as the manager, and the Pelicans moved their home games to the University of West Florida's Spooner Field. Quint paid $7,500 to lease the ballpark and cover the lighting and field maintenance costs. He also donated $500,000 to UWF to enhance the ballpark. The team averaged 1,000 fans in the new park but lost the championship to Baton Rouge.

The Southeastern League folded before the 2004 season, leaving the Pelicans without a league. Quint purchased the franchise rights of the Springfield Ozark Mountain Ducks, allowing the Pelicans to join the eight-team Central Baseball League. Travel became expensive, with the Pelicans playing five teams in Texas, one in Louisiana, and one in Mississippi. The Pelicans made the playoffs but lost the five-game series to the Shreveport Sports in the East Division Championship.

In 2004, Quint began searching for sites to build a baseball stadium. He said, "We needed to be financially sustainable. Spooner Field was too small; it's sort of out of the way. We didn't have parking, suites, or a VIP clubhouse."

Bonfield asked Quint to meet at Garden Street Deli. Quint recalled, "His concern was downtown and how to get companies to move into the City of Pensacola. Tom asked if I would ever consider building an office downtown."

The city manager played first base in the New York Yankees' farm system for one season. He and Quint started talking baseball. Quint said, "If I'm going to invest in a building downtown, I'd certainly like to talk about a ballpark downtown."

The conversation motivated Quint to have Mort and Miller explore possible sites within the city limits and near downtown. He needed enough space to construct a ballpark, an office building for Studer Group, and retail space to lease.

Quint hired Mike Thiessen, a financial advisor to Hall of Fame pitcher Nolan Ryan. Thiessen had helped create a dozen baseball parks, and his expertise was building financing packages to fund construction. He negotiated the deal that led to the construction of Dell Diamond in Round Rock, Texas, outside Austin. Ryan's Round Rock Express, the Texas Rangers' Triple-A affiliate, contributed $7.35 million toward the $25-million project and signed a 38-year lease for the 11,000-seat stadium.

"Someone mentioned the Trillium site as a possible site, but I cringed because of the crud surrounding the referendum in 2003," Quint said. "I didn't want to touch the property."

His advisors examined vacant property at the intersection of Main Street and Barrancas Avenue. It previously housed a restaurant that used railroad coaches as dining rooms. However, Mort discovered that a church had bought the site.

Quint, Mort, and Miller bounced around Legion Field as a possibility. In 1929, 3,000 fans watched the New York Yankees, featuring Babe Ruth and Lou Gehrig, win an exhibition game 12-5 at the ballpark, which was one block from West Garden Street. Legion Field had become home to the Southern Youth Sports Association's youth football league and was surrounded by houses, leaving little room for commercial development.

They shifted their focus to the American Creosote site on the city's west side, about a five-minute drive from downtown; however, the site had significant environmental problems. American Creosote Works treated telephone and power poles from 1902 until 1981, when the company filed for bankruptcy due to mounting environmental claims. In 1983, the Environmental Protection Agency added it to the Superfund program's National Priorities List. A temporary cap had been placed on the soil, but the site had not yet been fully remediated.

After discussing the site with engineers and city staff, Mort called Quint. "There's no way we can do anything with the site. We can't penetrate the cap."

The Trillium site became the default choice for the ballpark, but it had room for much more. Mort asked Miller to talk with Fetterman about incorporating the ballpark project with the maritime museum on the Trillium site, but the admiral wasn't interested.

"When I started talking to Jack about it, he lit up and told me that my grandmother was all sorts of things," Miller said.

Jack said, "We're not going to do that. We're not going to get in bed with (Quint). We got this maritime museum rolling. I don't know him, and he doesn't know me, and we will lose this if we aren't careful."

After the meeting at Cronley's and with Quint's blessing, Mort called Miller and asked him to intercede once more. The visionary project would go nowhere unless the architect could bring Quint and Jack together in the same room to hash it out.

A Gathering of Giants

The architect agreed to try. This time, Nancy Fetterman sat in on the conversation. "I went over to his house in Star Lake, but Jack still wasn't having it. Finally, Nancy said, 'Why don't you sit down and talk with Quint?' and Jack agreed to a meeting at my office."

Quint, Jack, Mort, and Miller were joined by Pensacola's top advertising executives—Dick Appleyard, head of the Appleyard Agency which handled Studer's marketing, and Ellis Bullock, whose E.W. Bullock & Associates managed the marketing for the Naval Aviation Museum and communications for the city.

Dick and Mort had been classmates at UWF. Dick said, "Accounting was our first class together. Mort went on to greatness in that field, but he was a unique bird in more than accounting and finance. Mort was a master at building relationships and could work a crowd. He was invaluable to Quint."

Jack presented his plans for the maritime park, and Quint talked about the stadium and his office building. Someone asked, "Could we combine the two projects on the Trillium property?"

"I didn't know Adm. Fetterman well, and I was sort of in awe," Quint shared. "And I said, 'First of all, I don't want to do anything that would hurt Adm. Fetterman's plan. This is really his call because I don't want to get in the way. After all, he is farther down the line with the museum than we are with this stadium.'"

What did Jack think? He said, "They fit perfectly. You have these two bookends that can support each other."

Mort recalled, "I'll never forget Adm. Fetterman, in the spirit of a Texas Hold 'em poker game, pushed his papers and notes into the middle of the table and said, 'Ladies and gentlemen, I'm all in.'"

Jack suggested adding another party to the project. He had talked with UWF President Dr. John Cavanaugh about the maritime museum being under the university and thought he might be interested. Mort had headed the search committee that recommended hiring Cavanaugh as the university's president in July 2002. He agreed that adding the university would make the project more robust.

In a few weeks, university officials proposed extending the campus downtown by relocating the history, marine biology, and archaeology departments to the park. The college would also pay commercial rental rates for classrooms and office space. The university's presence would also help attract matching state funds for constructing the maritime museum.

Miller was impressed by how well the two leaders connected. "Quint has such charisma that if you spend enough time around him, you suddenly start believing that by God, this might actually work. You find yourself saying things like, 'Give me a load.' Quint doesn't take a backseat, but he took a backseat to Jack. And that sealed the deal."

The architect worked on drawings that combined the two projects and added the UWF conference center. Miller said, "We did a master plan for the whole thing, showing all the parts and components we discussed. They reviewed it and said, 'Well, I think this could work.'"

City officials recommended bringing in Ray Gindroz and his Urban Design Associates at some point because the community gave him high marks for his 2004 study of the Seville Historic District.

"While trusting your intuition is important, it must also be supported by data," Quint recalled. "The question was, before we explore the possibility of a stadium on the waterfront, does this make sense? Gindroz had already established a good rapport with the community as a well-known urban planner."

Quint flew a group in his charter plane to meet with Gindroz at his offices in Pittsburgh. The baseball owner knew that the maritime park

41

plan would receive pushback from the public, and he wanted assurance that the project made sense to the respected, well-known urban planner. Gindroz liked what Miller had put together.

Appleyard joined Quint on the trip. "I remember he had a beautiful office from which you could see Pittsburgh's ballpark. Gindroz was a fascinating guy. But that trip was—I thought—*here's this guy, here's what he's done. He's going to help us do this.*"

While they traveled to Pittsburgh, Thiessen met with Bonfield and his staff to discuss how much the city could contribute to the project. For the 2003 Trillium project, the town had three state grant commitments totaling $5.7 million to cover the construction of a bulkhead, environmental remediation, and partial reimbursement for the land purchase.

Local Option Sales Taxes were considered a funding source but were dismissed because the tax required voter renewal every six years. Bonds would have to be issued to pay for the public sector contribution.

Meanwhile, Miller received a phone call from Mayor Emeritus Vince Whibbs. He heard about the project and wanted to get involved. Whibbs and his wife, Anna, were regarded as Pensacola's royalty. He served as mayor from 1977 to 1991, making him the longest-serving mayor in Pensacola's history.

Whibbs was a past president of the Pensacola Chamber of Commerce, Suburban Rotary Club, Gulf Coast Council of the Boy Scouts of America, and Junior Achievement. He was also a former board chair of Sacred Heart Hospital and AmSouth Banks of Florida. As an honorary U.S. Navy Blue Angels member, Whibbs received the Florida Bar Association Liberty Bell Award, Civitan Club's Citizen of the Year, and Silver Antelope for his service to the Boy Scouts.

He was famous for the greeting he used to open many events:

"Welcome to Pensacola, the western gate to the Sunshine State, where thousands live the way millions wish they could, where the warmth of our community comes not only from God's good sunshine but from the hearts of the people who live here. Welcome to Pensacola, America's first place city and the place where America began."

Miller thought, *My God, we have three of the most motivational people who can get something done in this town all synergized. This is going to blow and go.*

He was wrong.

Chapter 7:
Preparing for the City
Council

January 2005

The Maritime Park proponents set Tuesday, January 18, as the target date for unveiling their project publicly for the first time at the Pensacola City Council's Committee of the Whole.

Dick Appleyard explained their strategy. "Adm. Fetterman and Vince were the public faces because they added a lot of credibility to what we were doing. They were legends. Quint was the visionary behind the scenes, and the rest of us were there to help."

He added, "Quint had been successful at Baptist and was successful enough that he was respected. But he was new to the game."

Baptist Health Care Leadership Institute

Appleyard made a valid point. Although he successfully turned around Baptist Hospital five years earlier, Pensacola knew little about Quint Studer, except that he was a wealthy healthcare consultant who owned a struggling independent baseball team.

Why? Primarily because his office was across Pensacola Bay in the tiny bedroom community of Gulf Breeze, and Quint spent most of his time out of town with speaking engagements. However, there was another reason. Baptist Health Care had almost completely removed him from its website and marketing materials.

In 2000, Studer left Baptist Hospital but formed a partnership with the health care system, which announced him as the first president of the Baptist Health Care Leadership Institute. Baptist and Studer Group would split the profits from the leadership training and consulting business.

However, the partnership agreement was never finalized, and the joint venture only lasted a year after Baptist executives believed they would profit more by competing against Studer Group. The hospital changed its turnaround narrative, and the policies Quint initiated became known as "The Baptist Way."

The Birth of Rebuild

While Quint, Jack, and their team prepared for the Pensacola City Council meeting, Bankers Buzz Ritchie and Tommy Tait, builder Garrett Walton, Dick and Carolyn Appleyard, PNJ publisher Denise Ivey, and other business leaders formed the nonprofit Rebuild Northwest Florida to tackle the repair of homes damaged or destroyed by Hurricane Ivan. Their message was simple: "Help is on the way."

The leaders listened to the group from Homestead and established Rebuild so the full recovery burden wouldn't fall on local governments. Walton and Carolyn Appleyard agreed to serve as co-executive directors. In the News Journal's Sunday, January 9 issue, Walton stated, "The difference in what we are doing, as opposed to what Homestead did after Hurricane Andrew, is that it is coming from the hard-charging business community."

Tait added, "With proper coordination with the public sector, I think the private sector can play a major role in rebuilding Pensacola so we can be better prepared to withstand the next emergency that comes our way."

Rebuild initially focused on raising funds, assessing the needs of residents, particularly those without insurance, and establishing a construction company to handle the work. Ritchie and retired banker Eric Nickelsen led the fundraising effort. Retired Navy Captain Brian Watkins, the former commanding officer of NAS Whiting Field in Milton, volunteered as the construction effort manager.

Media Learns of the Plan

As the meetings approached, the city manager recommended that the maritime park proponents meet individually with council members to share project details.

"Not long after Miller created his first set of drawings, I made my first spreadsheet detailing how we would fund it," Mort recalled. "Bonfield recommended that we get in front of every council member, so we set up visits with each council member at Miller's office over three days. They came in, and we presented what we were trying to achieve, explaining that this was what we would propose in January."

"It was very positive until Marty (Donovan)," Quint said, "but we learned we had strong support from the other members."

Jane Birdwell joined the team. After spending ten years in Atlanta, she and her photographer husband returned to their hometown and launched Birdwell Photography and Marketing. Birdwell had done impressive work for the Florida Institute for Human and Machine Cognition, located in Pensacola's downtown historic district. Its founder, Dr. Ken Ford, highly recommended her to Quint.

She recalled how she was approached. "Mort and Quint knocked on my door and said they needed my help and wanted me involved. Quint's vision was to break building public support into big chunks, and I was put in charge of the forty-and-under crowd."

"We liked that a younger person was getting involved," Quint said. "Jane is the one who came up with the 'Right Idea, Right Time' stickers."

Mort and Quint asked Birdwell to tour the Trillium site with them. She said, "They told me to wear shoes that might get ruined. When I walked along the water and saw the bulkhead already in place, I thought, 'You've got to be kidding me. This has to happen. There's just no doubt we would be successful."

On Friday, Jan. 14, the News Journal reported that Studer, Fetterman, and Cavanaugh would present a bold plan for a public park, baseball stadium, and maritime park on the city's waterfront to the Pensacola City Council the following Tuesday. The projected cost was $70.7 million, with $31.1 million coming from the private sector. The public funding would come from a $40 million bond issue, similar to the Waterfront Festival Park proposal three years earlier.

Quint pledged $11.2 million, including $2.2 million in cash and $9 million in lease commitments for the ballpark and an office building on the Trillium site. Jack committed to raising funds to build the maritime museum. Dr. Cavanaugh agreed that UWF would use the accompanying conference center and naval museum to house its marine biology, history, and archaeology programs. The remaining private investment would come from the commercial and retail developments on the site.

The ballpark would seat 3,500 and could be used for various sports, concerts, graduations, and theatrical events. The left-field wall would be retractable, allowing the ballpark to open when events weren't scheduled.

Quint's office building on the site would house Studer Group. He agreed to host his firm's seminars in the conference center. He pledged to return any profits from his baseball team to the community and would pay a fair market rate for his use of the stadium and auditorium, as well as for the land lease for his office building.

Jack said the Maritime Park plan breathed life into his project. "The museum went into limbo for a long time, and then Quint Studer walked into my life."

Cavanaugh told the newspaper that he, Studer, and Fetterman presented an offer that city officials couldn't beat. "You've got an entrepreneur willing to move his company here, somebody with a big track record who is also planning to raise private dollars, and you have a university saying that we're really serious about being in Pensacola."

Councilman Jack Nobles praised the proposal. "This isn't coming from the city. It's coming from the private sector. We have a window of opportunity here. I'm very upbeat on it, and I support it 100 percent."

PNJ executive editor Randy Hammer agreed with Nobles. He wrote, "It would be a great way to put Ivan to rest."

Martini Night

Two nights before the PNJ article was published, Quint visited Global Grill, where our newspaper hosted a Martini Night.

Frank and Jane Taylor opened their tapas restaurant on South Palafox Street in early 2004. However, Hurricane Ivan struck just as they began building their business. The storm impacted the Taylors and our newspaper.

The Taylors' restaurant lost power and accumulated several inches of water. They were concerned about whether customers would return when they reopened. Hurricane Ivan shattered the windows of my office in the Thiesen Building, a historic five-story building half a block south of the restaurant. We needed electricity and internet access, so we rented a former yoga supply shop in Warrington on Pensacola's west side.

To ensure the Independent News maintained a downtown presence, I suggested we partner to host a Martini Night on Wednesdays at Global Grill. We would publicize the event in the paper, offer door prizes, and distribute flyers previewing the next day's issue. The Taylors agreed to provide drinks and tapa specials and pay for a musician to play.

We launched the first Martini Night on October 20, 2004. We created flyers and distributed them to the downtown offices that had reopened. We called friends and advertisers, inviting them to join us. The Global Grill bartenders crafted an "IN-tini" drink for the occasion. The mid-week social became a hit, reviving the restaurant and maintaining our newspaper's connection with downtown Pensacola.

Martini Night lasted for a dozen years. The Wednesday night crowd grew to nearly thirty regulars, and the event became a mid-week stop for Pensacola's movers and shakers. Additionally, people provided me with several news tips.

On January 12, Quint visited Global Grill out of concern that I might get upset if the daily newspaper published the plans before I had seen them. We found an open table so he could share the renderings of the maritime park and explain the basics of the plan. He said, "This is very similar to your ballsy plan."

Chapter 8:
Setting a New Course

January 2005

In the spring of 2004, my editor, Duwayne Escobedo, and I came up with the idea to create a downtown map that included all the projects community leaders had discussed for years but had yet to implement. The city had hired several consultants to hold workshops and produce studies, but it seemed to us that no one would ever pull the trigger on them.

The Metro Pulse in Knoxville, Tennessee, published a similar issue that generated considerable debate. We thought we could do the same, so we recruited David Alsop with Sam Marshall Architects and created our redevelopment plan for downtown Pensacola over beers and pretzels at Intermission, a bar across from the old courthouse. Duwayne dubbed it the "Ballsy Plan," which we published on May 2, 2004, under the title "Our Ballsy New Vision for Downtown P-Town."

The "Ballsy Plan" included a ballpark, maritime museum, UWF research center, convention center, entertainment district, new downtown library, botanical garden, outdoor amphitheater, hotels, and plenty of residential, office, and retail spaces. Our ballpark would also overlook Pensacola Bay from the end of Ninth Avenue, which was once home to Admiral Mason Park.

From 1956 to 1974, Admiral Mason Park, a 2,000-seat baseball stadium, existed at 100 South Ninth Avenue. It served as the home for three minor league teams affiliated with the Washington Senators and Chicago White Sox until 1962. The league folded because it refused to accept Black players, and the facility languished until the city demolished it in 1974.

Our proposed ballpark, Pelicans' Veterans Park, would seat 4,000 and have an additional fifty picnic spots on the outfield berm. It would anchor a multi-use development with a hotel, movie theater, and sports bar. The "Ballsy Plan" paid for it with a special-use district bond and estimated the cost at $6 million.

The proposed project that Quint shared at Global Grill on January 12 included several components of our plan. After he showed me the drawings and walked me through the proposal, I rushed back to our yoga shop headquarters and told my team to delay sending the pages to the printer. I rewrote "The Buzz" article to ensure we had something about the project in our January 13 issue:

Jump Starting Trillium

Two years after Pensacola citizens killed a $40 million City Hall boondoggle to build an auditorium and festival park on the prime 27-acre waterfront property, new plans are finally brewing.

Are you ready for this?

Retired U.S. Navy Vice Admiral Jack Fetterman, University of West Florida President John Cavanaugh, and Pelicans owner Quint Studer have been shopping around the idea of a maritime museum, marine research center, conference center, and minor league baseball park on the Trillium and adjacent 13-acre Bruce Beach property.

Pensacola City Council members and Pensacola News Journal bigwigs have gotten a sneak peek at the $70 million plans that will be unveiled to the public at the council's Jan. 18 meeting.

Talk about opening 2005 with a bang?

Each is pledging to bring money to the table for the development so that taxpayers won't be totally on the hook. City leaders, who already have invested $10 million of taxpayers' money into the prime property on Pensacola Bay along Main Street, are considering pledging another $3.8 million to the proposal.

The $3.8 million would come from an insurance settlement for Bayfront Auditorium damages suffered during Hurricane Ivan.

Whoa, say some insiders. City Councilman Marty Donovan, for one, says that money would be better served in restoring the auditorium to greatness.

Mayor John Fogg says the city has pledged to Palafox Pier developer and Network Telephone CEO Ray Russenberger to demolish the auditorium. Knocking it down is estimated to cost about $300,000. Once demolished, the city has proposed to build DeLuna Park on the site at the end of Palafox Street.

Don't expect the latest Trillium plans to be a slam dunk.

Independent News 2.0

Before Hurricane Ivan, our newspaper struggled to find its voice as we tried to earn a place in the community. In the storm's aftermath, the loss of ad revenue forced us to reduce our staff to three full-time employees, two part-time writers, and a handful of freelancers. We retooled the newspaper, focused more on investigative reporting, and sharpened our commentary.

We had a chip on our shoulder. The new, streamlined Independent News fought alongside its advertisers and readers to rebuild Pensacola, and we pledged to have "no sacred cows" and report whatever the facts revealed. If we failed, it would not be because we were timid and afraid to speak up.

The daily newspaper prospered. It had an army of editors, reporters, photographers, and graphic artists for its coverage. The News Journal capitalized on that advantage to cover the Maritime Park proposal in its Sunday edition with an editorial and four pages that included a double truck featuring an artist's rendering of the layout.

The PNJ interviewed Miller Caldwell, who emphasized the mixed-use component with funding from the public and private sectors. He believed the blend made greenspace possible on the site while also creating an economic catalyst by bringing baseball fans, tourists, UWF students, and others downtown.

"This is the type of engine that we need to help support the businesses downtown," he said.

Quint told the newspaper that he hoped the project would be completed by 2006, but city officials believed that 2007 or 2008 were more likely. He stressed that the stadium would have multiple uses, not just as a baseball park.

Councilman Marty Donovan stated that he would not vote for the project as presented.

"We haven't done the first thing first, which is setting aside the park on Trillium and Bruce Beach properties," he said. "We need to wait until we do some intelligent, comprehensive land planning on both those sites, and we haven't done that yet. The one thing that needs to happen down there before we can move forward is to have a firm, unequivocal pledge that the Main Street treatment plant would be no more."

Main Street Treatment Plant

The sewage treatment plant had blocked meaningful development west of Pensacola City Hall for nearly seven decades. The facility sat in the middle of the historically Creole neighborhood known as the Tanyard. Its license allowed it to pump twenty million gallons of treated effluent into Pensacola Bay daily. Worst of all, the sewage treatment plant stank, making it nearly impossible to move outside downtown when the wind pushed the odor toward Palafox Street.

The smell was so pungent that the Independent News created the Poot Index to warn residents about the dangers of walking outside on certain days. A score of less than four meant limiting exposure to five-minute intervals. A score between five and eight meant the air was unsafe for small dogs and children, and any score above eight could lead to possible death.

Most government buildings, schools, and facilities in Pensacola had been named after a city leader or politician. People called the facility sandwiched between Main and Government streets "Old Stinky."

In 1937, the City of Pensacola built two treatment plants, one on Ninth Avenue and the other on Main Street. In the mid-sixties, the Environmental Protection Agency recommended abandoning the Ninth

Avenue facility and expanding the Main Street plant. The plant underwent another significant expansion in 1977, doubling its daily capacity. Most of Escambia County's raw sewage flowed downhill to be treated on Main Street and then pumped into Pensacola Bay.

The Escambia County Utilities Authority was created in 1981 to buy the plant from the city to manage and expand the Pensacola and Escambia County water and wastewater systems. Under ECUA, more than $30 million had been spent on improvements, some of which added chemicals to the waste to eliminate the stench.

While some residents said the additives initially reduced the pungent smell, they soon found that the combined odor of the chemicals and sewage was nearly as overpowering. John Whittington, who lived across the street from the Main Street plant, told our reporter that he avoided sitting outside due to the sour smell lingering in the air most days.

"It stinks," Whittington said, standing on his front stoop and gazing at the plant when we interviewed him in October 2001. "They claim it doesn't stink. I'm down here every day. I was born down here. It doesn't smell every day, but it really stinks. It's not as bad as it used to be, but it still stinks. It'll always stink."

We published the story as the Pensacola Chamber began pushing for the Main Street Treatment Plant to be moved. ECUA Executive Director A. E. Van Dever pledged to spend an additional $3 million to address the issue. Still, he told the daily newspaper that he felt the plant was a convenient scapegoat. He claimed the most recent odor problem was only temporary and due to a mechanical malfunction. Van Dever expected the upgrade to make such malfunctions rare.

Chamber chair Mike Saxon stated that his group would not be satisfied with another band-aid. They wanted the ECUA board to answer questions about the cost, location, timetable, and funding required to relocate the plant out of downtown.

"We need to move forward instead of just talking about it," Saxon said. "It occupies prime property, and the chamber feels like it'll continue to be burdensome ecologically to downtown revitalization. ECUA can continue to work on it, but I don't know that they'll ever get it under control."

Van Dever responded with a letter to the eight most outspoken critics of the plant, requesting that each contribute $17,500 to pay for a study. ECUA board members discussed creating a ten-year plan to shut down the Main Street plant.

The relocation of the facility would continue to be debated for years. Our Ballsy Plan showed it removed and replaced with an aquarium and water park.

Hurricane Ivan intensified the need to relocate the Main Street Treatment Plant. FEMA funds were available, but would they be enough? On December 2, 2004, Governor Jeb Bush joined the initiative to move the Main Street Treatment Plant. He requested that FEMA allocate $40 million in federal funds for relocation instead of plant repairs.

In January 2005, we awaited news on whether additional federal funds would be available for what would become a $300 million-plus project to close Main Street and build a new state-of-the-art facility in central Escambia County. The plant's relocation loomed large over downtown's future and played a significant role in the Maritime Park debate.

Chapter 9:
Opportunity of a Lifetime

January 2005

When the Pensacola City Council held its Committee of the Whole on January 18, over 350 park supporters filled the council chambers. Many wore stickers that read, "Right Idea, Right Time." These stickers had been distributed during a pep rally at Seville Quarter the previous day.

Adm. Fetterman and Mayor Emeritus Whibbs addressed the council. Whibbs proclaimed, "This can change the face of Pensacola forever. It's the opportunity of a lifetime. Hurricane Ivan has devastated our town; what we need now is a little hope."

Appleyard recalled that the group had decided that Jack and Vince would have the most sway with the Pensacola City Council and the public. "Quint was smart enough to say, 'I don't have the credibility to present the project.' I don't know that many of us had ever even heard Quint speak at that time."

Laughing, the advertising executive added, "Here we had this asset sitting in the room that basically had an idea and money, but we didn't know he was one of the greatest speakers in the nation. We just thought he was a healthcare consultant."

The council liked what the two leaders presented. The Committee of the Whole voted 8-1 to place the item on the council's regular meeting agenda on Thursday, with Councilman Donovan as the sole dissenting vote.

Councilman Mike DeSorbo was out of town for the meeting. Two days later, at the council's regular meeting, he requested a reconsideration of the committee's vote so he could go on record as favoring the project. The motion for reconsideration passed 8-2; however, Donovan took advantage of the discussion to criticize the park supporters' motivations and methods.

"Obviously, while we were working on hurricane recovery, another group came up with their plan independent of us, city leaders," Donovan said. "My constituency read about it in the paper, and two days later, we have a well-orchestrated pep rally."

Thanks to Jane Birdwell, the Monday pep rally was well-orchestrated. She reached out to everyone on her expansive email list. The rally began with McGuire's Irish Pub's Bagpipe Band marching into the Seville Quarter's Phineas Phogg's dance hall. An excited mix of chamber leaders, Rotarians, and young professionals filled the room. Many later attended the Committee of the Whole and the regular council meeting, applauding Fetterman, Whibbs, and other pro-park speakers.

After the reconsideration vote, Donovan tried to get support for holding public workshops on what to do with the Trillium site and Bruce Beach, but not specifically for the maritime park plan on the agenda. The motion failed 7-3, with John Jerralds and Jewel Cannada-Wynn voting with Donovan.

Finally, the conceptual plan was approved, allowing proponents time to develop a more detailed plan outlining all the components, costs, and financing. The vote also gave city staff time to do their due diligence in evaluating the proposal.

However, several citizens expressed concerns during the meeting. CPA Charlie Fairchild, who had helped defeat the 2003 Trillium plan, asked the council to adhere to a public input process guided by city staff. He wanted a minimum of fifteen acres set aside for open space.

Fairchild's criticism surprised Quint because he and Mort had visited him at his office. Quint said, "We told him where we were going, just wanting to make sure he wouldn't oppose our plan. He basically said that he had done his one fight and wasn't doing it again. That felt good, but when we got before the City Council, all of a sudden, things started stirring up."

The Independent News staff attended the Seville Quarter pep rally, the Committee of the Whole, and the council meeting, and we walked away very impressed by the community's support and enthusiasm. In my

"Outtakes" column in the January 20 issue, I highlighted the difference between the Maritime Park proposal and the 2003 Trillium plan:

There will be naysayers who try to compare this new plan with the Pensacola city staff's waterfront festival park and city auditorium boondoggle, which citizens soundly rescinded in March 2003.

However, Trillium Trio's plan is significantly different from the last Trillium debacle. This new park proposal generates jobs, property taxes, and tourism dollars. It has plenty of public access and commercial space. Plus, the park foregoes any local option sales tax money.

Yes, it still contends with ECUA's smelly Main Street plant. But I'm willing to bet a whole case of Coronas that ECUA relocates the stinky dinosaur soon with federal and state aid. The public will not tolerate the facility downtown any longer after it spilled possibly millions of gallons of raw sewage during and after Hurricane Ivan. The sewage factory shouldn't derail this opportunity for an extreme makeover of Pensacola's old industrial waterfront.

In our "Buzz," we shared that the most significant negative we had heard was the lack of public input in the plan's development. We felt that the Pensacola City Council's unwillingness to listen to public suggestions had killed the 2003 Trillium proposal. Quint assured us that the proposal wasn't "set in stone," and the design would likely continue to evolve.

"We need all the citizens to share their ideas and concerns so that we can have the highest and best of this property," Quint told us. "What we wanted to do is get the ball rolling, and we are willing to commit our dollars to make it happen."

Little did Quint know that he would spend more than $1.2 million to win public approval.

Chapter 10:
The Gindroz Touch

February 2005

Before the end of January, Studer announced that he had hired Ray Gindroz to gather public input to develop the project's final design. While hiring Gindroz placated some critics, they would reserve judgment until the release of his report.

Councilman Donovan stated he would only be satisfied with a city-led, staff-driven plan for the waterfront. "I was the only council member throughout that Trillium effort who listened and spoke to the people on a daily basis. I know exactly what they want."

Our newspaper saw Quint's commitment to public input as encouraging, and we believed it would lead to more "buy-in" on what we viewed as a transformational project. I wrote, "We all have the opportunity to help improve the basic concepts and craft a development that will benefit the community."

But I also warned, "So many of us have gotten used to playing the devil's advocate on city proposals that we relish the fight more than actually achieving anything."

I felt that if the community didn't work together to improve the proposal, we might find ourselves five years later standing in line at yet another Walmart Supercenter, wondering what happened to our locally owned shops and restaurants and why our children can't find good jobs here.

Ray Who?

Architect and urban planner Ray Gindroz was an early pioneer of urban renewal, reinventing cities, and transforming urban communities. The bespectacled architect with a gray paintbrush mustache viewed urban design as an effective means to foster economic development.

His projects included Brooklyn Bridge Park in New York and downtown and waterfront plans for Norfolk, Virginia. Gindroz also taught urban design for over two decades at Yale University School of Architecture, Carnegie Mellon, and the City University of New York.

Pensacola became acquainted with him when the Florida Institute of Human and Machine Cognition (IHMC) and the local chapter of the American Institute of Architects invited him to speak as part of the IHMC Evening Lecture Series in 2002. IHMC founder Dr. Ken Ford met him through Robert Davis, the founder of nearby Seaside, Florida, which served as the backdrop for the movie "The Truman Show."

"His Urban Design Associates was the first architectural firm to focus largely on community building through architecture and urbanism, particularly in how the buildings relate to the street and other relevant issues," Ford said. "My reason for bringing Ray to Pensacola was that I felt the downtown had great potential. It had great bones, a good street grid, and a nice history, but it was underappreciated. I wanted him to advise us on the development of downtown."

In 1999, IHMC moved into the old Pensacola Police headquarters in the Seville Historic District, next to St. Michael's Cemetery. Ford believed that improving downtown Pensacola would make recruiting scientists easier.

After touring the downtown area in 2002, Gindroz told the lecture series audience that the economic value of waterfronts had changed because industrial uses were often not the highest and best use of waterfront property, adding, "The attraction that the waterfront has is irresistible for development."

He viewed the University of West Florida, Port of Pensacola, and IHMC as key players in remaking Pensacola's downtown core. Port activities enhanced the downtown's vitality and character. IHMC attracted knowledge-based workers to the area, and UWF owned twenty-nine buildings in the Seville Historic District.

Gindroz later returned to Pensacola and gave a presentation on the Seville Historic District's untapped economic and cultural potential. To develop a plan for its revitalization, he recommended a focused planning process that would involve three phases over five to six months and cost

$150,000. UWF and the city agreed to fund the plan, which Gindroz launched in August 2003.

Dr. Cavanaugh told the daily newspaper that the study would provide the university an opportunity to hear from the district's stakeholders. City Manager Tom Bonfield saw it as a catalyst. He said, "Let's have success before we jump into something else."

The Historic District public workshops were well attended. Participants agreed that the ECUA Main Street Sewage Treatment Plant should be removed, and that the industrial nature of the Port of Pensacola needed to change. They suggested adding waterfront shops and restaurants, more walkable sidewalks, a grocery store, and increased residential shade trees, parks, and museums.

Gindroz presented his plan in May 2004, the same month we published the "Ballsy Plan." The significant issues identified included the four lanes of Bayfront Parkway, the Interstate 110 off-ramp, and the Chase Street flyover, along with the need for clear entrances to the Historic District. The architect recommended more mixed-use developments, enhanced medians, and wider sidewalks, as well as more trees, underground utilities, and traffic-calming features.

The urban planner also advised that the city find ways to eliminate the unpleasant asphalt tanks at the Port of Pensacola and reduce Bayfront Parkway to two lanes as it passes through downtown. The lane reduction would make the waterfront more integral to downtown.

The News Journal editorial board praised Gindroz's plan and input-gathering process, noting the audience's enthusiastic response at the final presentation. The board added, "He has done his job, but now it's up to us."

Action Needed

Although he liked the Maritime Park concept, Gindroz didn't want to conduct another Pensacola study. When Quint asked him for help after the conceptual plan's approval, the architect expressed his frustration with the city leaders.

"You guys don't do anything," Gindroz said. "As an urban planner, the word 'planning' is in my title; you really want to see things happen. I've been there twice and haven't seen much movement."

Quint promised that this time would be different and agreed to pay the urban planner $200,000 to manage the public input process and develop a master plan based on that input. Gindroz and his team scheduled public workshops for the third week of February.

Meanwhile, Quint, Jack, Vince, Mort, and other plan supporters gave presentations to over two dozen civic clubs and community groups and appeared on six television and radio programs. The project had a logo and an official name, "Community Maritime Park," as well as a website, propensacola.com.

Quint hired the Market Research Institute to conduct an independent telephone survey. He explained, "I wanted an objective viewpoint. We are hearing great things from the community. I think this is part of our input process because not everyone can come to the meetings."

Councilman Donovan became furious, claiming the MRI poll failed to meet scientific polling standards. Our newspaper reported that the survey consistently indicated that nearly one out of every four Pensacola voters did not believe the city was moving in the right direction. They were dissatisfied with the performance of the Pensacola City Council and held an unfavorable opinion of the Community Maritime Park.

I wrote, "So no matter what the Trillium Trio proposes, nearly a quarter of the city will oppose it. The question is, will the city let this minority dictate what happens on this prime waterfront property?"

In mid-February, Bonfield brought in consensus-building expert Hans Bleecker to train staff on managing proposals and controversial projects to successful conclusions. Five days after the council vote in January, Bleecker spoke to about 175 people as part of IHMC's lecture series. He stressed that projects do not need the support of all residents, but successful leaders face critics head-on and work toward gaining acceptance of the proposal.

"Explore the full range of solutions," Bleecker said. "If people think you have a hidden agenda, they'll never trust you."

71

Quint attended Bleecker's lecture. "He said that successful projects are ones where the people who don't get their way still want what's best for the community, so they consent to be supportive. They want the project to succeed and agree not to sabotage it."

The city manager latched onto Bleecker's definition of informed consent—"even though not everybody agrees with the solution, at least people believe the process was fair." Could his staff help the community achieve informed consent for the Community Maritime Park?

While most council members were excited about the park, Donovan wasn't. In a viewpoint published in the daily newspaper, he claimed to have received emails and phone calls supporting his position that Trillium and Bruce Beach should be seen as one project. He advocated for an "open, independent process." Donovan argued that citizens should dictate how much of the property should be designated as a public park "in perpetuity" and that no funds should be committed to any project until ECUA relocated its Main Street plant.

"As a city councilman, I will continue to do everything in my power to initiate and foster an open and honest public planning process that is completely independent of any development proposal," Donovan pledged. "If we will allow this process to occur and we are willing to fully participate, the collective community wisdom that will emerge will result in a Community Maritime Park that will be the jewel of Pensacola's waterfront for generations to come."

Rebuild Raises Funds

While the city prepared for public input sessions on the Community Maritime Park, Rebuild Northwest Florida announced its fundraising successes weekly in the daily newspaper. Lamar Outdoor Advertising committed $250,000, while American Fidelity Insurance Company and the Homebuilders Association of West Florida donated $100,000 each.

Checks for $50,000 each poured in from WEAR-TV, Air Products and Chemicals, Inc., Levin Papantonio Family Foundation, Pensacola Christian College, AmSouth Bank, The Lewis Bear Company, Bud Light, Neal Nash, and the James J. Marks Foundation. Rebuild was well on its way to raising over one million dollars.

The organization also announced that Kenny Rogers would perform at a benefit concert for Rebuild on April 17, and Willie Nelson would also hold a fundraiser in either May or June.

Listening

On February 17, Gindroz held a series of small focus groups and conducted a forum to hear from all residents. Over 200 people attended and heard Gindroz express his tremendous enthusiasm for the project and the potential of the Trillium property. Some attendees wanted the architect to include Bruce Beach in his final report. He agreed to record the ideas but mentioned that they would not impact the Community Maritime Park plan.

One unenthusiastic participant was Councilman Donovan's wife, Helene. She said, "My initial reaction was that they designed a park around their buildings, not their buildings around my park."

Gindroz announced his timetable: in mid-March, he and his designers would return to meet with the public to refine the details. He would give a final presentation in April. He stated that the development should not be delayed by any decision to relocate Main Street plant.

"His philosophy was if you wait for the plant to move, nothing will ever happen," Quint recalled. "If you start putting the right project stuff close to the plant, it'll force the discussion to take place, and the pressure to move the treatment plant would increase."

However, the Letters to the Editor disagreed. One reader wrote, "No, no, no. Let's not fall for this. Four years from now, as the stink interrupts our picnics and ball games at the new $70.7 million ballpark, we'll be saying to ourselves: 'I sure fell for that.'"

Another suggested conducting a survey of the Pensacola residents. "I believe they'll find that a substantial number of people would opt to move the sewage plant before spending $70 million on the park."

In the following weeks, town hall meetings were held with the council members in six of the seven city districts. Only Donovan refused to host one, casting a shadow over Gindroz's work.

Would any study please those who defeated the Trillium proposal two years earlier?

Chapter 11:
Dollars & Cents

March-April 2005

As March approached, the UWF Haas Center for Business Research and Economic Development released its analysis of the proposed plan's economic impact. The Haas Center estimated the Community Maritime Park would generate about $51 million annually in new economic activity, including 767 new jobs with an annual payroll of $24.1 million.

While Gindroz worked on the park's master plan, Mort collaborated with city staff to iron out the project's budget and financing. On March 7, Bonfield outlined the park's financial plan to the council's finance committee.

The Community Redevelopment Agency would issue bonds for what it could not secure in grants to cover the city's $40.7 million share of the $70.4 million project. Taxes generated within the CRA would be used to cover the bond payments. The private sector would contribute $29.7 million.

Park Cost Breakdown

Construction

Site development costs	$8,250,000
Stadium	$11,200,000
Maritime Museum	$10,000,000
UWF Conference/Learning Center	$7,875,000
Studer Office Building	$7,500,000
Private Development, retail	$4,250,000
Parking Garage, 500 spaces	$5,000,000
Breakwater and marina	$2,500,000
Total	$56,575,000
Design and related costs	$5,774,625
Project-related costs	$2,400,000
Contingency	$5,657,500
Grand Total	$70,407,125

News Journal columnist Mark O'Brien called the Community Maritime Park "Trillium II." He criticized the city council for being "so busy praising the plan, they have raised few questions."

The notable exception was Donovan, who told O'Brien, "I don't have the luxury to jump on the bandwagon."

The councilman was concerned about the $37 million in interest he estimated the bonds would cost. He wanted to slow the process down by seeking an official appraisal of the Trillium site. "I think the citizens need to know what the property is worth."

O'Brien worked for Ellis Bullock in the 1990s as a spokesman for the city after leaving the daily newspaper around 1989. PNJ executive editor Randy Hammer brought him back to write four times a week about "what really goes on in town." Having that much column space in the daily newspaper had a significant influence on O'Brien's community. The columnist became a consistent critic of the park and a window for Donovan and others to bash the project.

On March 10, the City Council voted 7-1 to proceed with the Community Maritime Park plan. Donovan dissented, Councilman J. D. Smith abstained because his daughter worked for Studer Group, and Mayor John Fogg missed the meeting due to illness. The approval was subject to the council's future approvals of the site plan, funding, development agreement, and operational agreements.

At the meeting, community advocate Byron Keesler objected, claiming that the council's vote rendered public input meaningless. He accused Studer of lobbying the city to build offices on the most expensive land in town while expecting taxpayers to construct a ballpark for him. Fairchild suggested that the ballpark would better fit at the port than the Trillium site.

Donovan claimed the residents' reaction was "extremely negative." He argued that the plan would take funding away from renovating the downtown library and other projects. The councilman said, "There are more questions than answers."

The following week, Gindroz and his design team shared sketches and received feedback from the public in four two-hour interactive sessions over two days. The designers had shifted the office buildings and parking garage off the waterfront to connect the park to downtown more effectively. They also suggested extending DeVilliers Street across Main Street through the property and ending with a wharf with docking space for charter boats and water taxis.

After those sessions, Gindroz presented his outline for the park to about 150 people in Pensacola City Council Chambers. The new configuration offered 18 acres of open park space—nine times the size of Seville Square. Most attendees praised the latest design, though some expressed concerns about handicapped access, hurricane vulnerability, and vehicle access for festivals.

Quint said, "It is beyond what I ever dreamed."

Mayor Emeritus Whibbs called the design "incredible" and praised the team for holding so many public meetings. He added, "Don't ever tell me that you didn't have a chance to be heard."

The Vagabond Newspaper

While the city waited for the urban designer to return with his final plan, the Independent News lost its office in Warrington.

"Rick, Navy Boulevard is flooded. The water is heading right toward your office," my landlord shouted over the phone during a torrential downpour around 9 p.m. on Wednesday, April 6.

When I arrived at our temporary office, a narrow building between the Psychedelic Shack and Domino's Pizza, water filled the space up to my knees. I heard computers beeping. With the help of the Psychedelic Shack staff, I unplugged computers and lifted them off the floor. Water poured out of the metal casings, and papers floated everywhere. The only dry spots were the desktops. It was just as devastating for our newspaper as Hurricane Ivan.

We later determined that a county road crew had cleared debris in a nearby neighborhood but failed to remove the tree limbs. The remaining debris clogged the storm drains and worsened flooding in the already water-saturated area.

Thanks to businessman Robin Martin's generosity, we set up a temporary office in the storage area in the back of his Distinctive Kitchens showroom, next door to Global Grill. At the same time, we waited for the renovations of a space on Palafox Place to be finished. I had signed the lease before the rainstorm.

Miraculously, most of the equipment still worked. However, it took a day for us to clean up the old swampy office and move our dwindling possessions, which my staff moved in a U-Haul truck while I attended my father-in-law's funeral in Greenville, Mississippi.

I wrote our readers in the April 14 edition, "During the past six years, we have battled fire, wind, famine, and now floods. Bring on the locusts. No biggie."

Master Plan Delivered

On the same day that Independent News issue hit our newsstands, Gindroz presented his Community Maritime Park design to the Pensacola City Council. It included the DeVilliers Wharf, a 3,500-seat multi-use stadium for baseball and outdoor events, a conference center with a ballroom and meeting area, a maritime museum and UWF research center, mixed-use office and retail buildings, and about twenty acres of public park space with natural conservation areas, a bayfront promenade, and a festival place.

Gindroz wanted the park to have a neighborhood feel. Quint recalled, "He didn't want a big museum. He wanted a museum that would look like a waterfront fishing village. He didn't like giant buildings, preferring smaller ones that were more adaptable to changes in the market. He had a little town square with a clock."

At the presentation, the urban planner said, "This will represent an enormous increase to your tax base. This master plan sets up the framework for development and human activity."

By a 9-1 vote, the Pensacola City Council approved Gindroz's design. Again, Donovan cast the dissenting vote. Though extensive public input had been sought and incorporated into the design by a renowned urban planner, the critics still weren't satisfied.

More hurdles were on the horizon as Quint's team and a city official hammered out the details of implementing Gindroz's master plan.

Chapter 12:
A Long Hot Summer

May 2005-June 2005

As Memorial Day weekend approached, PNJ columnist Mark O'Brien suggested the Pensacola City Council rethink the Community Maritime Park and ask developers nationwide if they had a better offer for "a project that has more appeal to the public and less cost to the taxpayer."

He echoed Donovan's comments about needing a site appraisal. He argued that less than half an acre, located two blocks east of Trillium, with hurricane-damaged buildings and no waterfront access, sold for $1.5 million. O'Brien wrote that selling the site across from City Hall for upscale housing would provide a better deal for taxpayers.

"There's no need to rush into a deal now," the columnist wrote. "Better to wait until this fall when the community is scheduled to learn what will happen to the downtown's biggest blight, the Main Street wastewater treatment plant."

He expressed concern that the city might need the $40 million earmarked for the Community Maritime Park to help ECUA relocate the Main Street facility. "If the city borrows the money for the park, it loses its ability to borrow funds to move the plant. Then, the city could have a great park but a ticking time bomb of a sewer plant barely a block away—not the correct priorities."

Field of Schemes

In June, the CRA held a public hearing on amending the Community Redevelopment Agency Plan to identify the Community Maritime Park project as the specific project targeted for the Trillium site. Bonfield explained that the amendment informed the public that the property would be available for redevelopment. He didn't expect the project's final approval until fall, and construction would likely begin in late winter 2006.

Since February, Quint's attorney, Bob Hart of Clark, Partington, Hart, Larry, Bond, and Stackhouse, had been meeting with the city's attorneys on the actions needed for the CRA to approve the park's master plan and any bond issuance. They determined that Florida law mandated the plan amendment.

For this book, Hart shared how his firm came to represent Quint. When he and Baptist Hospital were negotiating his employment agreement, hospital officials warned Quint not to hire the Clark Partington law firm.

"So, what'd he do? The person he initially went to was Dennis Larry, my partner," Hart recalled. "Dennis helped Quint negotiate that contract.

I don't know how many years later—three or four years—he returned to Dennis and said, 'I'm leaving. I'm going to start my own company.' Dennis told him, 'You need to talk to Bob.' That's how my fascinating ride with Quint began."

In June 2005, Councilman Donovan attempted to prevent the public hearing with a motion at a council meeting to seek proposals for different ideas regarding the site nationwide. Ignoring the months of public meetings and town halls, he stated, "Most decisions are made behind closed doors. Politicians are lobbied behind closed doors... Maybe we can set a new tone."

In the public forum, Fairchild labeled the Community Maritime Park proposal a "field of schemes" to build a "subsidized baseball park and conference center." He also targeted Quint during council meetings.

"One City Council meeting, I was sitting there, and Charlie got up, looked at me, and took his wallet and put it in his front pocket like I was a pickpocket," Quint recalled.

Donovan's motion failed, but his and Fairchild's comments and their insinuations of impropriety angered Mayor Fogg and Councilman P.C. Wu.

"If you have something, you come forward and put it on the table, but I'm not going to sit here and be a punching bag and take it," Wu said.

Mayor Fogg said, "There is no reason to impugn the reputation of this City Council or Bonfield and his staff. I'm getting sick and tired of it."

The meeting upset Quint and his "brain trust." Every Friday morning, Jack Fetterman, John Cavanaugh, Miller Caldwell, Mort O'Sullivan, Ellis Bullock, Dick Appleyard, and Bob Hart met to share updates on the project. Depending on his schedule, Quint would attend in person or by phone. They decided to respond to the insinuations after the council meeting.

"As it began to come clear that Marty and his followers were never going to consent to the plan, our concern was if we had another referendum, Marty and his group would have a tremendous advantage," Quint said. "They had all these names of those who signed the Trillium petition. We had never been through this before and needed to come out and play offense."

He added, "We wanted Marty and Charlie to know we weren't just going to sit there and be silent."

Two days after the vote to schedule the hearing, Quint ran a print ad with the title "Nothing Could Be Farther from the Truth," responding to Fairchild's "field of schemes" barb and Donovan's implication that council members were making decisions "behind closed doors."

In the ad, he called their remarks "discouraging and disappointing". He praised Fetterman, Cavanaugh, and the others helping him improve the community's quality of life as a "team of like-minded, respected, honorable individuals."

Quint said, "Our critics have willfully misled the public about the park. And others have been personally attacked, and the plan has been characterized as a 'scheme' that is somehow meant to defraud. It's shameful."

He pledged to keep pushing forward. "Let's not let a few hold us back. Let's continue to work toward making Pensacola the best it can be."

Firestarter

As summer approached, I set out to profile Quint Studer and Charlie Fairchild, whom I considered the central figures in what might become a battle over Pensacola's future.

Quint's son, Mike, and my daughter, Tricia, graduated from Gulf Breeze High School a year apart, but I didn't know much about Quint's personal story until he invited me to fly with him to Boston to hear him speak.

In the article "Firestarter," this is how I described the opening of his presentation:

People slowly fill the ballroom of the Seaport Hotel in Boston. It's Saturday morning, and the group looks like it could use another couple of hours of sleep. These are college professors on the third day of the annual conference of the Association of University Programs in Health Administration. About 200 educators made it out of bed to listen to the keynote speaker, Quint Studer, CEO and founder of the Studer Group.

On the edge of a raised platform at the front of the conference room sits a short blonde man in his early 50s wearing a brown suit, navy blue shirt, and tie. He smiles to himself at the fact that no one, not even Ph. D.s, likes to sit in the front row.

Upon introduction, Studer springs to life, jumps onto the platform, and begins speaking.

As he revs up, he removes his coat and places it over an empty chair in the front row. Studer says, "Sometimes I must calm down because I get too excited. I remember when Lynyrd Skynyrd was coming to my local town. I was so excited I bought all their CDs and learned all their songs—' Who's That Girl,' 'That Smell.'"

The audience laughs. "By the time Skynyrd came to town, I was too exhausted to go to the concert." The room roars with laughter. Already, he has won over this crowd.

Studer spends the next hour relating personal examples about how to change the culture of any organization and how these teachers can help their health administration students bring excellence to prospective healthcare employers.

His enthusiasm is contagious, and his sincerity, humility, and passion shine through. The room is awake now and hangs on every word, nodding their heads in agreement. One can almost see light bulbs popping on above their heads.

During the return flight, Quint openly shared his past failures and how he hit rock bottom and turned his life around. He answered every question without hesitation, and I saw what Marty Donovan and Charlie Fairchild missed. Quint had been bullied throughout his childhood, but he would not let Pensacola's naysayers intimidate him.

He believed the Community Maritime Park would be a catalyst for improving the quality of life for all citizens, and he wasn't going to back down, no matter how badly Donovan and Fairchild tried to smear him.

I found a kindred spirit in Quint, and our newspaper would do whatever it could to combat the false narratives bubbling in the city.

Packed Chambers

On June 23, citizens packed the council chambers for the public hearing on amending the Community Redevelopment Agency Plan for the Community Maritime Park.

Jane Birdwell had developed a knack for organizing rallies and packing council chambers. She recalled, "I had never seen such mass passion. We drew the crowds by asking each person to bring two others. I was taught that everyone has someone in their life who will feel equally passionate about a project, so it's an easy task."

The pro-park attendees arrived jazzed from a pre-meeting tailgate rally held on the City Hall property. Supporters of all ages united in the belief that the proposed development was precisely what the town needed. They loudly voiced their support for Quint, Mort, and others who spoke at the rally. Quint reiterated his personal and financial commitment to the project, drawing the loudest applause. Mort corrected the inaccurate economic impact claims that opponents were circulating.

Jason Crawford, a former UWF Student Body President and a 2004 graduate, pointed out that most UWF students choose to move to other cities for better job opportunities right after graduation. The energy generated by this plan has given them a sense of purpose and pride in being part of a community they can call home.

During the council meeting, Councilman Donovan drew laughs when he said, "No one wants to see this property developed more than I do."

The chuckles were so contagious that Mayor Fogg had to bang his gavel to restore order. The other park opponents bombarded the proposal with complaints about the CRA, odors from the Main Street sewage treatment plant, and inner-city crime, but none of their arguments swayed the council.

Ultimately, the council voted 9-1 to amend the CRA Plan to identify the Maritime Park project as the specific project targeted for the site. Mike Wiggins, P.C. Wu, and Mike DeSorbo were the most vocal Council supporters. Donovan cast the lone vote against the project.

Critics called the plan self-serving for the developers and a waste of money for a city still recovering from Ivan. Others chastised Fetterman, Studer, and Cavanaugh for not being developers. The council continued to hear that people wanted the Main Street plant removed before any development on the Trillium property.

Opposition to the Maritime Park began to organize publicly. Fairchild told the daily newspaper he was meeting regularly with a small group of residents who believed the design wasn't what was promoted. Donovan said he wanted the developers to start from scratch and develop new plans for the site.

Though few wanted to admit it yet, Pensacola was heading for another referendum battle. The tension would continue to mount as the proposal's specific details unfolded and the Pensacola City Council prepared for its final vote on the project.

Chapter 13:
The Opposition Solidifies

July 2005

On July 1, we celebrated our newspaper's sixth anniversary. Editor Duwayne Escobedo recapped how we survived the past ten months.

As Hurricane Ivan approached Northwest Florida in September 2004, we finished our IN Music Awards issue. We moved our computers to the center of the Thiesen Building's third floor before heading home, expecting the storm to pass us by.

"Only Hurricane Ivan spanked us hard that Thursday instead," Duwayne wrote. "We put a paper out in a darkened Thiesen Building running on backup generators."

My editor continued, "We moved and put a paper out in the only powered-up, Internet-connected office we could find, near the corner of Navy Boulevard and Gulf Beach Highway. Sure, we battled a gnat swarm, endured a sieve of a roof, and watched police mop up a murder across the street."

He covered our relocation to Distinctive Kitchens after the April flood and how we published the newspaper despite sporadic wireless Internet service and only three cell phones. The editor pledged that we would continue "making fun of humorless local politicians, blasting boneheaded moves, pushing the envelope, fighting for the underdog, and scrapping with the powers that be."

My Open Letter

In our anniversary issue, I wrote an open letter to Donovan and Fairchild, asking them to put down their swords and work toward consensus. "No matter how strongly one believes in a position, there comes a point when one must step aside and admit there's no support on the council or in the community for your views."

I explained that we had joined them in opposing the 2003 Trillium plan because it had many deficiencies, such as a lack of job development, no commercial or retail space, and no addition to the tax base. The Community Maritime Park plan addressed our concerns.

"Marty and Charlie, it's time to move on, work positively for the Community Maritime Park, and come to the table with open minds," I wrote. "This is a good time to build consensus and find common ground to proceed. Instead of constantly looking for what's wrong, look for what's good and help improve it."

Charlie Fairchild

Fairchild didn't listen to me but eventually agreed to an interview. After reading Studer's profile, the chairman of a new political action

93

committee, Save Our City, was eager to discuss his opposition to the park.

The certified public accountant served as the senior partner of Fairchild & Baniakas, CPAs and Business Advisors, which had been established in downtown Pensacola since 1969. His first office was in the San Carlos Hotel, a historic building known as the "Gray Lady of Palafox" that had been demolished for the federal courthouse.

He was a part-owner of the now-defunct Pensacola Continental Basketball Association team, the Pensacola Tornados. Fairchild also invested in several restaurants, small service companies, and software development firms.

In addition to being a board member and past officer of the Florida Institute of Certified Public Accountants at the local and state levels, Fairchild had been involved with the Fiesta of Five Flags, Economics Club, Panhandle Tiger Bay Club, Five Flags Rotary Club, Pensacola Seville Sertoma Club, and Pensacola Exchange Club.

He served as co-chair of Citizens Against Trillium, which opposed the 2003 Trillium plan. In 2004, he unsuccessfully ran for Pensacola City Council District 7, losing a run-off to Jewel Cannada-Wynn by 231 votes.

On the eve of Hurricane Dennis in mid-July 2005, we sat in his Blount Building office overlooking downtown Pensacola. We discussed his opposition to the Community Maritime Park and what he preferred for one of the last large tracts of undeveloped land on Pensacola Bay.

"I realize that there needs to be some type of economic development to support the park," he said. "I would be satisfied with 200 feet along the waterfront and five acres on the peninsula dedicated as public parks."

He didn't believe that the University of West Florida needed a "trophy waterfront location." The accountant felt its downtown campus could be built anywhere. "Professor offices, classrooms, and administrative offices can be located elsewhere."

Despite the Pensacola Chamber and the hospitality industry clamoring for a conference center, he said it wasn't needed. He said, "What we need is a replacement for the Bayfront Auditorium."

He particularly disliked the baseball park. "I don't care what the park's promoters say. It's not a mixed-use facility. Other events may be held there, but they will only be taking them away from other venues."

Fairchild liked the maritime museum but wanted it at the Port of Pensacola. "The museum should be an anchor for downtown. I don't consider Trillium property an anchor. The Port of Pensacola is a natural location for the museum. It's close to the Historic District. Other museums are within walking distance. Building the maritime museum is a great way to preserve the Port of Pensacola."

He participated in Gindroz's input sessions but was disappointed in the final plan. "The park promoters hired him, so he brought them a plan that gave them what they wanted."

Fairchild also defended his assertion that the project wasn't a public-private partnership. "The taxpayers of Pensacola are paying for the public park, baseball park, and conference center. The private sector is paying for its buildings. I don't consider someone building their building part of the public. The original proposal had the private sector putting $2.25 million towards the public sector, but that has gone away. It cannot be a public-private partnership unless the private sector is paying part of the public's $40 million."

The accountant said Save Our City had yet to decide to push for another referendum, but he did think the issue was heading in that direction. "I don't see the process changing. The Pensacola City Council is so locked in that they aren't open to hearing any other proposals."

He wanted the city to issue a new request for proposals, advertise it nationally, and give developers six months to respond with their best ideas. "Then, the City Council could truly look at what's best for these 27.5 acres."

Quint's Cash Contribution

I asked Quint about Fairchild's complaint that no private funds were going to the stadium or conference center. He said he initially intended to put $3 million into the project.

"Because of interest rates and construction costs, I thought I could build the Studer Group office building for $8 million and needed 10 percent down, about $800,000," Quint explained. "The remaining $2.2 million would help pay for the stadium's construction."

However, his advisors shifted the $2.2 million to the maritime museum during one of its Friday meetings that he didn't attend. The state had a program matching large contributions to state universities. Since UWF would run the museum, Studer's $2.2 million would double.

"Anyone would say, 'Let's move this money to the museum because it became worth $4.4 million.' So that's what we did," Quint said. "When I came back, I told them I supported what they did, but it's going to be a real public relations challenge."

Quint was right.

Chapter 14:
Hammering Out Details

August 2005

Studer, Fetterman, and Cavanaugh formed Community Maritime Park Associates (CMPA) to officially respond to the Request for Proposal for the park's development. Throughout July, Mort, Miller, and attorney Bob Hart met with development consultant Barry Abramson and financial advisor Mike Thiessen to determine the construction budget, finances, and each party's commitments.

In a viewpoint in the Pensacola Business Journal, Mort presented the CMPA proposal the group had developed, which had been tweaked since the March council meeting and modified to fit Gindroz's master plan.

The city's $40 million from bond issuance would construct the necessary infrastructure for the property, including the public park, conference center, and multi-use stadium. The funds would also cover the site work for the maritime museum. These developments would encompass approximately twenty acres.

The CMPA committed to private development in two phases. In the first phase, the CMPA committed $30 million in cash contributions to build the Maritime Museum, the Studer Group office building, and a mixed-use commercial and residential space. The second phase would build out the project as Gindroz envisioned. The fully developed private investment would approach $60 million.

UWF would own the $15-million maritime museum, and the construction would be funded by $7.5 million in private donations and an equal amount from the state's Cortellis matching grant program.

The bonds would not be repaid from the city's operating budget or with local option sales taxes. Instead, the CRA tax revenue would make the payments.

The CRA was established in 1982 to promote economic development and urban revitalization in the area bound by Bayfront Parkway, A Street, Cervantes Street, and Ninth Avenue. To fund the CRA, the county approved a tax increment financing fund (TIFF) and committed any real estate tax revenue growth from 1982 forward to the CRA district.

Under Florida law, the CRA could only use the TIF funds to revitalize the district and not be used outside the CRA or for General Fund expenses like police and fire. However, it is an effective way to bootstrap a community into redevelopment and revitalization.

The CRA TIF grew from $60,000 in 1984 to $3.4 million in 2004. Over the previous five years, the revenue growth had averaged 24 percent per year, thanks to improved property values and new development.

Mort predicted that the growth in CRA tax revenue over the next three decades would far exceed the $70 million needed to pay the principal and interest on the bonds. Using city staff's conservative estimates of 10 percent growth over the next fourteen years and 5 percent after that, the CRA was projected to collect more than $385 million over the bonds' 30-year lifespan. The CRA would have more than enough money to repay the bonds, contribute to the relocation of the Main Street treatment plant, and fund other projects in the CRA.

In the proposal, Quint Studer pledged to:

- Contribute $2,250,000 for the construction of the Maritime Museum.
- Build an $8 million office building and relocate his staff to Pensacola. He would assist his employees with down payments if they moved within the city limits.
- Conduct monthly healthcare conferences in the UWF conference center. At the time, Studer Group hosted such sessions nationwide, generating more than $2 million annually in food and beverage revenue for the conference centers. The conferences would produce over 10,000 bed nights annually for local hotels.
- The Pensacola Pelicans committed to a ten-year lease at $175,000 per year.

- All Pensacola Pelicans profits would be donated to local charities, and Quint would not receive any salary or fees. For the first five years, he pledged to donate a minimum of $250,000 annually to charitable causes.
- Jack Fetterman committed to raising the funds to build the Maritime Museum. UWF promised to:
- Own and operate the Maritime Museum.
- Lease an entire conference center floor for classroom and office space at more than $300,000 per year.
- Move its archeology, marine science, and history programs to the park.
- The CMPA agreed to:
- Attract more than $7 million in additional private investment, including 34,000 square feet of mixed-use space, during the first phase.
- Develop the remaining phases of the property as market conditions permit, resulting in over 150,000 square feet of mixed-use and residential space.

Covenant for the Community

In August, Quint addressed two dozen Black business owners at a Gulf Coast African American Chamber of Commerce network session.

He said, "It's important in our view to have the Black community's full participation in a project that is vital to the rehabilitation of the city's west side."

Oliver Darden, a former Indiana Pacer who owned several Burger Kings in the Pensacola area, was excited because no one had ever asked the Black community and other minorities to participate actively in a major city project. "This project opens up investment opportunities, improvement, and growth to the west and north, reaching areas like historic Belmont-DeVilliers, where we need that kind of economic boost."

Realizing he needed more than the support of Black business owners to win a referendum, Quint sought out civil rights leader Leroy Boyd. The sixth of nine children of a truck driver and a maid, he worked for almost three decades as a machinist at the Navy Depot, eventually becoming the director of the manufacturing division. In 1997, Boyd retired when the Navy closed the facility and founded Movement for Change to fight racism, injustice, and inequality in Pensacola.

Boyd was a problematic, uncompromising figure who frustrated leaders of all backgrounds. When the Pensacola City Council twice rejected his request to name a city street after Dr. Martin Luther King, Jr., he organized a boycott of Pensacola businesses. His supporters picketed Horizon Bank, Cordova Mall, and the Pensacola Chamber offices. The council relented and renamed part of Alcaniz Street for Dr. King by a 6-3 vote in June 1999.

When the number of citizens killed by deputies began to mount, Boyd and Rev. Al Sharpton's National Action Network called for a July 4 protest on the Pensacola Bay Bridge. Sheriff Jim Lowman got them to call off the protest after holding a five-hour meeting with Boyd and community leaders. Boyd also started another fight with the Pensacola City Council over the Confederate flag flown as part of the City of Five Flags display.

Boyd opposed the 2003 Trillium plan because the construction contract only set aside $700,000 for Black-owned subcontractors. Quint wanted to assure him that more business would go to minority-owned subcontractors. He met with Boyd and his board at the Movement for Change's Center for Social Justice.

Quint felt he had earned credibility with the Black community. "When I was president of Baptist Hospital, I promoted the first Black nurse manager, Lynn Pierce. Our facilities department was all white, and our housekeeping department was all Black. We stopped that and integrated the departments."

Studer committed that the maritime park would create jobs for minority groups. "I thought it was going pretty well. And then Leroy said, 'Well, how do we know this will happen? And I said, "Because I'm giving you my word." But that wasn't good enough for Leroy. He wanted it in writing, which eventually became the Covenant for the Community."

The document became a contract with the community that the maritime park would be a "catalyst for a better today and tomorrow for the people of Pensacola."

The CMPA board would mirror the city's demographic diversity.

A Contractor Academy would be established to educate and assist local and minority contractors. The subcontractors also would reflect the city's demographics, with a particular focus on attracting minority-owned companies. Support services, from security to maintenance to accounting, legal, and advertising, would also match the community's demographics. Every effort would be made to ensure that activities for city youth, such as sports, educational, and recreational camps, would be offered free of charge or with scholarships for those in need of assistance.

Bye, Blue Angels Classic

On August 18, Pensacola suffered another loss when the Blue Angels Classic, formerly known as the Emerald Coast Classic, announced that the Senior PGA Tour event would be played at Sandestin, a resort an hour east of Pensacola in Okaloosa County.

NBC Sports reported, "The move likely signals the end of professional golf in Pensacola. The Pensacola Open, which began in

1929, was the oldest Florida stop on the PGA Tour until it was discontinued in 1988, also due to financial issues."

The financial problems stemmed from the lack of sponsors to cover the larger purses required by the PGA. Pensacola was part of the Nike Tour for a few years, but it didn't gain much traction.

In 1995, Jimmy Lee, the CEO of Buffalo Rock, a soft drink distributor in Birmingham, Alabama, launched the Emerald Coast Classic as part of the Senior PGA Tour. Eight former Pensacola Open winners participated in the first tournament. Over the next decade, the tournament faced struggles with weather issues, schedule changes, and the challenge of meeting increasing financial demands.

At Jack's recommendation, the tournament was renamed the Blue Angels Classic in 2004 to capitalize on the popularity of the Navy's flight demonstration squadron and attract Boeing as a sponsor. Unfortunately, Hurricane Ivan's destruction, followed by Hurricane Dennis less than ten months later, cut off local sponsorship dollars as businesses focused on rebuilding. South Okaloosa County had the funds and appealed more to Boeing.

The relocation announcement strengthened my resolve to support the maritime park. I wrote, "Instead of community leaders rallying to keep it, they simply held the door open for the departure. If we don't build the Community Maritime Park and develop other ideas to revitalize our area, we will have to accept that Pensacola's day has passed."

Sewage Plant Progress

On August 25, Baskerville-Donovan engineers presented a site plan proposal to the ECUA board to demolish the Main Street treatment facility and build a state-of-the-art facility on 327 acres owned by Solutia in northern Escambia County. The construction timetable depended on how quickly ECUA could raise $165 million.

ECUA received $13.6 million in state and federal grants and secured a $24 million low-interest state construction loan. The board hoped that the city and the Escambia County Board of Commissioners would contribute to the new plant.

Downtown Pensacola would no longer have to endure the stink from the Main Street plant, and Pensacola Bay would be healthier without daily discharges of treated wastewater. ECUA Executive Director Steve Sorrell told the media that the Solutia site gave ECUA unlimited expansion capability. The board members liked the plan and placed it on the agenda for the September meeting for final approval.

Hurricane Katrina

That same day, Hurricane Katrina struck southeastern Louisiana and Mississippi. We watched thousands on the Interstate highways attempting to flee New Orleans as the storm approached and intensified. Most of New Orleans and neighboring parishes were flooded for weeks.

Thousands who did not evacuate were stranded without electricity, food, or water.

Hundreds of evacuees made Pensacola their home. Escambia County coordinated local, state, and federal agencies to provide them with services. Hurricane Katrina reminded many Pensacola residents of how vulnerable the city's waterfront was to hurricanes. Some began to have cold feet about building a stadium on Pensacola Bay.

Chapter 15:
Dollars Get Tighter

September 2005-October 2005

The Katrina catastrophe prompted retired UWF finance professor C.C. Elebash to write a viewpoint asking the Pensacola City Council to re-evaluate the Community Maritime Park project. He questioned the Haas Center's economic impact study. He argued that the benefit of relocating Studer Group's employees to the park was overstated by $8 million because only twenty employees would be moving from outside the area.

Elebash also thought the museum was too small to attract 350,000 visitors annually, even though Fetterman believed it would lure about a third of the Naval Aviation Museum's one million visitors. Though Quint spoke to packed auditoriums around the country, the retired professor felt that the projection of 200 events averaging 900 attendees was not credible due to the "intensely competitive" conference center industry.

The multi-use stadium was significantly larger than Pelican Park at UWF, but Elebash dismissed its claims of attendance growth, stating, "Minor league baseball is a local attraction. It does not draw many people or money from outside the area."

He presented the Pensacola City Council with two options: either build a minor league baseball park or relocate the Main Street Wastewater Treatment Plant. There was little doubt about what he wanted them to choose.

I responded in our newspaper, "ECUA can pay for the $167 million relocation and construction of a new plant within its rate structure for as little as $6.75 per month for its residential customers. The CRA can pledge its revenues to finance a bond issue for the park development. We can and should do both."

Plan Retooled Again

In October, the park proponents faced the reality that construction costs had risen by 12 percent after Hurricane Katrina. Several project features would have to be deferred, including the trellis skirting the outfield wall, breakwater, gazebos, and picnic shelters. The conference center needed to be reduced from 22,500 square feet to 15,000 square feet, which still made it one and a half times larger than the city's largest meeting venue, New World Landing.

Opponents saw an opportunity to halt the project. Councilman Donovan said, "I think the city is waking up to the reality of this more and more. How is the city really benefiting from this park?"

He added, "The idea was cut before the public was ever aware. That's the way they do things around here."

Bonfield scheduled a public workshop in late October for the council and public to hear the capital budget, overall project costs, construction timeline, projected operating budget, the term sheet of the proposed deal with CMPA, as well as the private development prospects and potential revenue from private investments.

At the Committee of the Whole on October 24, Elebash reiterated his complaints about the UWF Haas Center's economic impact study. Dr. Rick Harper, the head of the Haas Center, defended the report. The UWF economist conceded that a more miniature maritime museum could reduce the number of visitors. However, Harper felt that the number of Studer Group employees was irrelevant because he based the payroll impact on the building's square footage.

Councilwoman Jewel Cannada-Wynn wanted a new study from another source because she believed the Haas Center had a conflict due to the university's involvement in the project. Mayor John Fogg agreed and wanted the Haas Center to assess the economic impact of the proposed changes.

The public workshop was held the following day. Nearly 200 people filled the Bayview Senior Citizens Center for over three hours. They wore blue or yellow stickers to show their support or opposition to the project. The council and public learned the stadium construction budget had increased from $11.2 million to $15.7 million. The breakwater, marina, and parking garage would have to be built in a second phase.

Unpopular Watchdog

After Hurricane Ivan's anniversary, tension grew in both our community and newsroom. We had stepped up our watchdog coverage, and while our papers were flying off the racks, our financial situation showed only modest improvement.

Our readers valued our reporting, but we faced constant resistance from government officials and business leaders. The weeks following Ivan saw us investigating insurance adjusters who lowballed claims, exposing contractor scams, and documenting the dysfunction in our courts. My "Outtakes" column took on a sharper edge. We were all hurting—our readers and us—and we fought for the truth.

Throughout 2005, we didn't take our foot off the pedal. We broke the story about Pensacola Police's excessive Taser use on suspects, including releasing video footage of a prisoner being tasered in the county jail. This reporting drew national attention to Taser abuse in Escambia County, though it certainly didn't endear us to law enforcement.

When former County Commissioner Willie Junior was found dead under a house, just a month before his court date, we covered more than just the official press conference. Junior had testified that former commission chair W.D. Childers had given him a collard greens pot filled with roughly $100,000 to vote for $6.2 million in county land deals—

testimony that led to Childers' bribery conviction. Officials ruled it suicide and tried to quash alternative theories, but we reported on why many in the community weren't convinced.

The Humane Society of the United States brought us another major story—hog-dog rodeos, where pit bulls were set loose on feral hogs. Their four-month investigation had led to several arrests, and they shared exclusive footage that we published online. These stories built our readership but didn't exactly attract advertisers.

As our community watched Mississippi and Louisiana rebuild after Hurricane Katrina, questions arose about Rebuild Northwest Florida. The nonprofit was created to help low-income families in Escambia and Santa Rosa counties repair their homes quickly after Hurricane Ivan. However, hundreds of homes still had blue tarps for roofs, even though Rebuild had collected $1.9 million in donations and received a $1 million federal grant.

In June, the media requested financial statements and inquired about the slow pace of repairs. The nonprofit attributed the delays to an over-reliance on church volunteers. They announced new arrangements with professional roofers and promised to repair 150-200 roofs monthly starting in July.

The story took a turn in September when the Santa Rosa Press Gazette revealed that Rebuild had approved $1 million in salaries back in April, according to a leaked internal document. Rebuild officials claimed it was just a draft and denied paying any executive salaries.

The nonprofit held a press conference to address the renewed call for financial statements. The event felt more like a pep rally, packed with donors, staff, and their families. Seeing the Pensacola News Journal Publisher Denise Ivey on stage, I knew we were in for a rough ride. After several speeches, they announced that the release of the financial statements would wait until after the annual audit.

I should have recognized the warning signs, but I pressed on. After the rally, I wrote that their limited disclosures failed to answer the public's questions. I argued that the only way to refocus the community's attention on Rebuild's important work was through complete financial transparency.

Rebuild invited me to their October monthly meeting—the only journalist among fifty nonprofit and business leaders. The executive director shared a detailed management report covering staffing, construction, and finances. The board approved several transparency measures: creating a PR Committee, publishing board minutes and financial reports online, and holding regular press sessions with co-executive directors.

We published the financial information and reported on their new transparency commitments, though some felt I could have handled the situation more diplomatically.

When most publishers would have retreated to safer coverage, I intensified our investigative reporting. In October, Movement of Change president Leroy Boyd alerted me to a death at the Escambia County Jail. Robert Boggon, a 65-year-old truck driver, had been arrested for disorientation and knocking over store merchandise. In his confused state, he resisted arrest, leading to charges of aggravated assault and criminal mischief.

Inside the jail, Boggon's mental health deteriorated rapidly. He spat at staff, refused meals, and desperately called for help. Rather than providing mental health care, corrections officers repeatedly tased him, used pepper spray, covered his head with pillowcases and towels, and administered sedatives that left him in a stupor.

Eleven days after his arrest, Boggon was found dead in the infirmary, naked, and strapped to a restraint chair shortly after being tased in the shower. After my editor published the story, we joined Boyd's protest march. Nearly 200 people demonstrated outside the sheriff's office and jail, demanding justice while Sheriff Ron McNesby's deputies photographed the crowd.

McNesby attempted to use these photos to pressure my investors, demanding a retraction and my editor's termination. At an investor meeting, he displayed a picture of me at the protest, challenging me to explain myself.

"Can I have a copy?" I asked. "This is a really good photo of me."

This enraged both McNesby and my investors. They pressed me on what it would take for the Independent News to write more favorable coverage of the sheriff's office.

Rising from my chair, I said, "When he quits killing people, our coverage will change," and walked out.

In the following ten months, two more inmates died in custody, and McNesby would lose his reelection bid two years later.

The county sheriff thought I was a fool, and within a month, I had antagonized him, my investors, and Pensacola's business community, proving that he probably was right.

Chapter 16:
Prelude to the Vote

November 2005-December 2005

With the final vote on the horizon, the battle over the Community Maritime Park moved from Pensacola City Hall to the opinion pages of the local newspapers.

C.C. Elebash characterized the Community Maritime Park proposal as an $800,000 subsidy for Studer's baseball team. He arrived at that figure by stating that taxpayers would pay about $1 million annually on the interest and principal of the $16 million borrowed for the stadium. Then he deducted the amount that Studer would pay to rent the baseball facility.

Councilman Donovan sent an open letter to Quint and Fairchild, calling for a referendum on the Community Maritime Park. If voters did not approve the park, the city would hold a new round of public input followed by a nationwide request for proposals. He wanted to create the impression that he had no relationship with Fairchild or Save Our City. We would later learn otherwise.

Quint and Fairchild's reactions were predictable. Quint felt that each delay led to more young people leaving our community. He said, "You can't just keep waiting for one more thing—another meeting, study, or vote."

Fairchild liked the idea, adding it was the best way to avoid the "bitter fate" of the 2003 Trillium proposal. "The longer this thing waits and festers, the worse it's going to be."

Pensacola Young Professionals

While Studer discussed the importance of keeping young talent in Pensacola, our newspaper began meeting with young professionals in the Pensacola Chamber's conference room to see if they would be interested in banding together and speaking out on issues.

The meeting happened because I challenged the Pensacola Bay Area Chamber of Commerce in my "Outtakes." My daughter, Cat, shared her frustrations since graduating from the University of Florida and returning to Pensacola. She was tired of being dismissed and told to wait her turn whenever she tried to speak up at a meeting. The chamber took pride in its three-legged view of its mission: armed forces, tourism, and economic development. I wrote that a few young professionals wanted to work at NAS Pensacola, wait tables, or answer phones at a call center. The chamber's stool didn't give them a leg to stand on.

Chamber CEO Evon Emerson felt that I didn't understand what her organization was doing for the community. When I visited her office, I thought I would have a short conversation and receive a scolding.

Instead, she took me to the chamber conference room, filled with her department heads, and had me sit through ninety minutes of presentations on their programs.

When they finished, I shared the conversations I had with Cat and her friends. They were fed up with hearing leaders talk about young talent but not inviting them to the table to listen to their voices. To my surprise, Evon listened. We didn't agree on every point, but we both recognized that the status quo had to change. We decided that a partnership between the Pensacola Bay Area Chamber of Commerce and the Independent News could be a catalyst.

Hurricane Katrina delayed the process, but in November, we invited a small group of young leaders to meet and discuss the possibility of organizing a group that would serve as a networking tool and help voice their generation's opinions and ideas to the community leaders.

Their enthusiasm, intelligence, and openness floored us. Evon and I found their candor, sincerity, thick skins, and lack of hidden agendas refreshing. We asked them to return in December, bring a friend, and be prepared to work out the details.

That nucleus would become the Pensacola Young Professionals. After each meeting, we asked the attendees to bring a new person to the next one. By March 2006, the group was ready to go public. They would play a significant role in the passage of the referendum.

Field of Dreams

In our cover story on November 8, "Field of Dreams," we explored whether the waterfront stadium would increase the Pelicans' attendance, spur economic development, and be used for purposes other than baseball games.

During the 2005 season, the Pelicans' attendance at the remote University of West Florida baseball field averaged more than 1,600 fans per game. The team conservatively projected a nightly average of 2,338 baseball fans at the Maritime Park, generating about $1.73 million in revenue against $1.49 million in expenses.

Eighty cities had built baseball stadiums for affiliated minor leagues and independent leagues since 1992. Studies indicated an increase in overall attendance, especially for minor league teams that remain in the same city.

The Charleston RiverDogs saw attendance skyrocket from 100,428 to 231,006 when it opened the Joseph P. Riley Jr. Park, or "The Joe," on the banks of the Ashley River in 1997. The Appleton Timber Rattlers increased attendance by 174 percent in its new digs in 1995.

Independent minor league teams like the Winnipeg Goldeyes and Sioux Falls Canaries also saw attendance jump. Winnipeg crowds swelled 56 percent to 248,488 in 1999, and Sioux Falls attendance rose 14 percent to 135,216 in 2000.

Mayors informed us that the downtown ballparks spurred economic development. The mayor of Brockton, Massachusetts, Mayor John Yunits Jr., credited the city's $17 million ballpark as a key factor in helping transform the industrial, gritty, crime-ridden town. The city's assessed taxable property rose from $2.6 billion to $6.6 billion over the past few years.

Mayor Joe Riley Jr. took pride in his city's 5,900-seat baseball stadium. Charleston residents turn out to the $20 million stadium, which hosts the Yankees' Class A affiliate, the RiverDogs, for concerts and festivals.

"People said, 'Why go to the expense of building a baseball park on the river?' The answer is found at the baseball park now," Riley said. "It is the thousands of families who go there to one of the most beautiful sites in America, in their city, not in some faraway place, enjoying a memorable experience."

TYYO

At the end of November, the Studer Group held a seminar titled "Take You and Your Organization to the Next Level" at the Hilton Garden Inn on Pensacola Beach. Quint chose Pensacola to demonstrate he could fill an auditorium.

The Hilton Garden Inn conference room was packed with 300 people from thirty different states and sixty-five organizations who flew into Pensacola to hear him speak about the Studer Group's management tools. The attendees filled hotel rooms at the Hilton and the nearby Spring Hill Suites.

I attended the seminar and spoke with the participants. In my "Outtakes," I wrote, "The two-day seminar validated for me that the Studer Group can attract visitors to Pensacola, especially in the off-season. The product it offers is substantial and has staying power. It's definitely an asset to the community."

Jack Pushes Back

As the negative letters to the editor in the daily newspaper mounted, Jack voiced his frustrations in a viewpoint. He also responded to rumors that he had lost enthusiasm for the maritime museum.

The retired admiral had been sidelined "due to some medical challenges" over the past three months. In September, he had surgery to treat diverticulitis, an intestinal disorder. He later had another surgery on his ankle, which put him in a wheelchair when he made his daily visits to the Naval Aviation Museum.

He wrote, "I assure you that I am even more enthusiastic and motivated about the maritime museum and waterfront project than I was when I initially presented the plan before the City Council."

Jack believed the park opponents had resorted to attacking leadership because they lacked credible facts to dispute the project. He asked why they questioned the motivations of "well-meaning, highly motivated, experienced, and trusted leaders" like Quint and Dr. Cavanaugh.

The admiral wrote, "It is the right project at the right time."

Chapter 17:
The Council Vote

January 2006-March 2006

As we entered 2006, city officials wanted to temper expectations for when we would see the first pitch in the new stadium. The first baseball game probably wouldn't happen for four years because of the lengthy federal and state development permitting processes, environmental remediation, and construction.

The master development agreement was scheduled to be presented to the council on January 12. However, the CMPA group requested that the commission wait so that the development agreement and proposed lease could be voted on simultaneously.

On January 31, Gannett announced that Kevin Doyle, the publisher of the Oshkosh Northwestern, would succeed News Journal publisher Denise Ivey, who had been promoted to the publisher of The Courier-Journal in Louisville, Kentucky.

Doyle covered the San Francisco 49ers during the Joe Montana era for Thomson Newspapers. He was also president of the community-owned Wisconsin Timber Rattlers in Appleton, a Class A affiliate of the

Seattle Mariners. He quickly advocated for the Community Maritime Park.

PACE Awards

On February 7, the chamber held its Pensacola Area Commitment to Excellence (PACE) award ceremony. Quint received the Community Leader Award. In his acceptance speech, he challenged the chamber members to begin working immediately to make Pensacola the best place to work, play, and live in the country.

Quint couldn't find the speech for this book, but he recalled the gist of it. "I acted like I had discovered a New York Times article from 20 years in the future, and I found an article that talked about how we became the greatest city in America. And the journey began with the Community Maritime Park."

Jack received the Pioneer Award, which had been presented only nine times since 1978. The award coincided with his announcement of retirement from the Naval Aviation Foundation on March 22 to spend more time with his wife, Nancy.

Rebuild Northwest Florida received the "Spirit of Pensacola" award. Executive director Garrett Walton told the audience that his group would not rest until it finished its task despite vast obstacles.

Stadium Challenge

I received several emails from readers who criticized the baseball park as unfeasible. I responded to each one, defending the park's feasibility.

One email shared an article questioning the economic impact of the Montreal Expos' relocation to Washington, D.C. It also quoted a study on thirty-seven major metropolitan areas with major league baseball and football teams, highlighting some of their problems.

Another focused on the Florida State League. According to the email, the league reported an average attendance of 1,279 fans per game. The emailer asked, "Can any league expect to survive with this lack of support? Will it be different in Pensacola?"

I argued that the Pensacola Pelicans averaged over 1,600 fans at the University of West Florida last season. New minor league ballparks in other cities led to increased attendance, so there was no reason to assume the Pelicans' attendance would decrease to the Florida State League level.

I sent park opponents a list of minor league teams in Southern cities—all averaging more than 2,000 fans each game in 2005. I asked them to pick out five teams in metropolitan areas with similar populations and ballparks built in the past five years. We could jointly study those teams and let the chips fall where they may. If they suggested any other minor league teams with new ballparks, we could include them in the analysis, too.

No one accepted my challenge.

Park's 'Price Tag' Inflated

In a letter to the editor, Elebash jacked up the cost of the "Trillium Maritime Park" to $100 million. He wrote that the city would borrow $42 million, pay $40 million in interest, and provide $20 million in waterfront real estate. He said, "Nearly 50 percent of the $100 million will go to two perilous ventures, the ballpark and a conference center."

Elebash added that any discussion of the stadium being used for anything other than baseball was unrealistic.

LeaP Fireworks

Fireworks ignited when the Leadership Pensacola (LeaP) Class of 2006 had architect Brian Spencer, Mort O'Sullivan, Charles Fairchild, and Councilman Marty Donovan debate the Community Maritime Park.

Established in the fall of 1982 by the Greater Pensacola Chamber, LeaP helped cultivate talented leaders and orient them on community issues and how state and local government operated. Each LeaP class consisted of fifty participants, representing a diverse cross-section of area businesses and organizations. The classes engaged in a comprehensive ten-month program consisting of retreats, day-long seminars, and visits to the state capital and several local government agencies.

In the meeting, Fairchild angered the group by suggesting that decisions about the city's future should be left to its elders because they possessed the necessary wisdom and experience.

LeaP member and PYP co-founder Jenni Pate responded, "It was your generation that thought putting a sewage treatment plant in downtown Pensacola on Pensacola Bay was a good idea."

The LeaP class continually pressed Fairchild for his ideas for the Trillium property, if he could do anything he wanted. He wouldn't answer the question. Instead, he kept repeating his view that the people should be heard.

Donovan didn't escape unscathed, either. The councilman told the class that he wasn't opposed to the maritime park but criticized the process. He believed that the city didn't follow proper procedures and policies and didn't get sufficient public input.

After the fiery discussion, the LeaP class voted 46-1 in favor of the Community Maritime Park.

USS Oriskany

At the Pensacola Chamber board meeting in early March, Jack announced that the USS Oriskany would be sunk in the Gulf of Mexico on May 17. The EPA had given its final approval in February.

Jack joked, "To all those disbelievers who said this would never happen, I accept your apologies."

The Oriskany was another of Jack's initiatives. He led the effort to have Escambia County selected as the site for the USS Oriskany to be used as an artificial reef. The date had been moved several times because of hurricanes and government red tape.

During the Vietnam War, the Oriskany launched nearly 20,000 combat sorties. Several pilots who became Naval aviators at NAS Pensacola were shot down and taken prisoner in North Vietnam, including Jack's buddy, Sen. John McCain, for the aircraft carrier that played a significant role in the Korean and Vietnam wars. The Oriskany had been decommissioned and sat idle since 1976.

Florida won a competition against Texas, Mississippi, South Carolina, and Georgia for the aircraft carrier. Recognizing the vast tourism value of the artificial reef in attracting thousands of divers, Escambia County pledged $1 million, and the Navy allocated $2.8 million for the project.

The Oriskany would become the world's largest artificial reef, 25 miles off Pensacola Beach. It arrived in Pensacola on Wednesday, March 22. Two days later, Jack died at home.

The Big Vote

On Monday, March 27, the Pensacola City Council convened as the Community Redevelopment Agency and opened with a moment of silence in honor of Fetterman.

Mayor Emeritus Vince Whibbs asked those favoring the maritime park to stand, and most of the overflow crowd did. He told the council that the park would be a "catalyst" for downtown's renaissance and "define who we are and what we are."

PYP board member Ashley Hodge spoke in favor of the project and introduced PYP officers and board members. UWF President John Cavanaugh read a message from Nancy Fetterman: "We deeply believe in this project, and we have worked to make it a reality because we believe Pensacola deserves nothing but the best."

Save Our City's Charlie Fairchild said his group wanted a referendum on the project. "We're still confident that a referendum is going to allow the people to have a say in such an important issue."

The Pensacola City Council voted 9-1 in favor of the project. Donovan cast the lone dissenting vote.

While it seemed inevitable that Save Our City would push for a referendum, Mort remained positive. "We've reached a milestone in this effort, and we look forward to making it a reality."

The next day, Save Our City announced it would begin a petition drive.

An Irish Wake

On Wednesday, March 29, hundreds gathered at the Fetterman's home to celebrate his life with an Irish wake. Guests were greeted by McGuire's Irish Pub Pipe Band, playing "Anchors Aweigh." Bishop John Ricard presided over his funeral mass at the Pensacola Naval Air Station chapel the following day.

David Hartman, former co-host of "Good Morning America," gave one of the five eulogies. He talked about how Jack "revived our spirits whenever he was in our presence. He oozed intelligence, compassion, integrity."

I used my "Outtakes" to pay tribute to Jack:

Bye, Jack.

Pensacola lost its strongest advocate and most selfless leader on Friday, March 24, when Jack Fetterman died quietly in his Star Lake home.

Jack was a retired three-star vice admiral and the former head of Naval Education and Training Command at NAS Pensacola. He recently retired as president/CEO of the Naval Aviation Museum Foundation. In 2000, Jack was president of the Pensacola Bay Area Chamber of Commerce.

He was also my hero and one of the most admired in this community.

A recent poll revealed that the three most respected persons in the Pensacola area were Pensacola Mayor Emeritus Vince Whibbs, banker Buzz Ritchie, and Fetterman. Just in case you're wondering, my name comes up way down the list after the guy who rides around Pensacola on a bike covered with Mardi Gras beads.

Pensacola is entering a new age as Generation X (30-40-year-olds) and Generation Y (18-29-year-olds) are beginning to seek a more active leadership role. Read the letters to the editor in our paper, and you'll see the gray hairs are upset and are quick to mock them.

Jack would've never reacted in such a way. He welcomed younger leadership. Jack may have fit better in Pensacola Young Professionals than in his age group. He always took on new challenges and pushed others to make his adopted home better. No problem was too difficult or issue too thorny for Jack to tackle.

At an age when most people are cutting back on their activities, Jack fought through pain and illness to serve his community. While many of his fellow retired naval officers spend most of their day worrying about their tee times and golf handicaps, Jack was on the phone calling military and political leaders on behalf of community projects.

Jack refused to follow the lead of so many of his peers, who fight nearly every project that has the potential to help Pensacola grow and improve. Instead, he blazed new trails and was constantly thinking of new ways to revitalize this area.

In just the past five years, he led an effort by the Naval Aviation Museum Foundation to build the National Flight Academy; successfully helped to get the USS Oriskany as an artificial reef off our shores; joined the Community Maritime Park effort to make a maritime museum on Pensacola Bay; and worked tirelessly to garner national support for the Blue Angels Golf Classic.

Jack helped accomplish countless other smaller projects behind the scenes. I relished working with him on an idea and listening to his enthusiasm as he described a no-nonsense approach to achieving it.

I believed in his leadership and knew that if Jack were behind it, the project would be completed.

Along with countless others, I will miss Jack Fetterman. In some of my darkest hours of trying to publish a newspaper that challenges the status quo, Jack was always there to offer advice and listen to me vent.

I recall one function we both attended that was filled with county commissioners, city council members, and government officials, most of whom I had upset in the paper's latest issue. Jack chuckled as I walked by and softly said, "You better stand by me before somebody slugs you."

For the next hour, Jack made sure they shook my hand as he greeted them and subtly let it be known that he supported me.

Pensacola will miss Jack Fetterman. This is a much better place because of his leadership, and I'm a better person for having known him.

There would be no better tribute than to name the Community Maritime Park after him. Fetterman Park. I like the sound of it. Let's make it happen.

Pensacola stood on the precipice of its second referendum fight in the city's history, and Quint had lost a crucial voice for the project. Who would step up to help?

Chapter 18:
Sides Chosen

April 2006

Save Our City selected four sites to collect petition signatures: the recycling bins on Summit Boulevard, the closed Exxon station at Ninth and Bayou Avenues, Cordova Mall, and the Barnes Supermarket near downtown. A door-to-door campaign would focus on the predominantly white neighborhoods east of Ninth Avenue.

The News Journal reported that Save Our City's objections to the park stemmed from their belief that the planning process lacked adequate input from residents and that the city didn't seek other proposals.

Those gathering signatures were told to "hit and run"—not to educate or debate the public. "If they won't sign in the first thirty seconds, move on."

The group had sixty days to present the signatures to the city clerk. The clock started on March 28, which made the deadline to present the signatures Friday, May 27. The executive committee would hold the signed petitions until May 26 to force the city to conduct a vote-by-mail election. The same strategy had worked three years earlier with the first petition drive.

Save Our City announced it would hold weekly meetings at 6 p.m. on Tuesdays at the Bayview Community Park Senior Center. Because Fairchild and Donovan had accused Quint, Mort, and the city officials of developing the maritime park plans behind closed doors, the PAC announced all meetings would be open to the public.

Mort's young partner, Jeff DeWeese, took them at their word and showed up to each meeting, providing me insights into their strategies and progress with the petition drive.

Name-calling was standard fare. The Independent News became a "rag," and the park supporters the "Community Maritime Pirates." The Pensacola Young Professionals were "young Turks," whom they described as "very polite, very knowledgeable but misguided by their employers."

They singled out Mayor Emeritus Vince Whibbs and me for their scorn. At the time, I served on the Gulf Breeze City Council. Save Our City members questioned why I wasn't distressed about the Studer Group relocating from Gulf Breeze to the Community Maritime Park. Shouldn't the Gulf Breeze City Council fight to keep the company?

While the threshold to force a referendum was 5,547 signatures from registered Pensacola voters, Save Our City set a goal of gathering 8,000 signatures to survive signature challenges. Typically, about 30 percent of the signatures on any petition did not qualify and were rejected by the

135

Supervisor of Elections. In less than two weeks, the group had collected about 1,800 signatures.

Fairchild sounded confident when he talked to the daily newspaper. "I think we're better engaged this time around, and that has put us ahead of schedule."

Save Our City did have an advantage over the park supporters. Quint recalled, "We were concerned that they were prepared. They had all these names from the referendum in 2003. They also had Mark O'Brien and Luke McCoy, top media personalities with significant influence, in their corner."

Jeff DeWeese

Quint had Jeff DeWeese, who fearlessly met Save Our City head-on. He grew up in Pensacola and graduated from Woodham High School. He played linebacker on the football team that won twenty-eight regular-season games and two state championships. Fairchild's son Geoff was a teammate.

"I had known Charlie Fairchild my entire life. I went to elementary, middle, and high school with his son, and we played football together," Jeff said. "We have always, even through this, maintained a civil relationship. We could always talk about what's going on with the families."

When Hurricane Ivan hit Pensacola, Jeff and his family lived in Germany, where he worked for General Electric (GE). He said, "We listened to Ivan on the internet radio from Germany, and we knew how bad it was."

GE wanted him to move to Schenectady, New York, but he and his family decided to return to Pensacola, where Jeff accepted a job with O'Sullivan Creel.

"Maren and I went on a house-hunting trip to Schenectady, and GE said, 'Well, we're going to put you in temporary housing until the spring so that you can actually see what your yard might look like with grass,' which didn't excite us," Jeff recalled. "Mort had always left the door open. When we came home for Christmas before we moved, I went and met with him, and that's when the decision was made."

Mort immediately assigned him to Quint Studer, the Pensacola Pelicans, and the maritime park proposal. Quint was a very significant client of O'Sullivan Creel. He was still in a little office in Gulf Breeze and spent most of his time on the road. Mort asked me to help the baseball team. I was with the baseball team for years as we set up front-office operations."

As he became more involved with the Community Maritime Park effort, the young CPA became concerned that the firm might question his lack of billable hours. "Mort basically told all his partners, 'Don't bug him about his chargeable hours. He's on this project.' So, I was all in on the maritime park."

The accountant took a crash course on municipal finances to determine how the CRA could pay the bonds for the maritime park and help ECUA relocate the Main Street Plant. "I never knew much about municipal government before that. I had to learn how the city government works and where the financial information was."

ECUA hired O'Sullivan Creel to work on how the city and county could pay something toward the plant relocations.

"We met with each council member, City Finance Director Dick Barker, and all the county commissioners. That's when I learned what walking the halls was," Jeff said. "We needed to get commitments on what each of them would contribute toward a new $300 million plant. Part of that was Mort handing me the City of Pensacola's financial report for the previous year, which was about three inches thick. He expected me to find the money so that we could tell Barker where it was, program by program."

Jeff also attended the weekly meeting at Miller's office, where Quint, Mort, Jack, John Cavanaugh, Bob Hart, Dick Appleyard, and Ellis Bullock discussed the latest developments. "As the concept came along and we knew that there was going to be a big pushback, we would meet and give me my tasks for the week— 'Okay, this is what you're working on right now.'"

And, of course, he attended Save Our City's Tuesday meetings at the Bayview Community Park Senior Center. "Everybody always knew after the council passed the project in March that the Save Our City folks would do a petition drive for a referendum. This was their entertainment. They liked getting together on Tuesday nights and rail at the project and us."

Worthy Opponent

PYP quickly became a viable counter to Save Our City, something Donovan and Fairchild didn't have to deal with in the 2003 Trillium referendum fight.

Over a hundred young leaders gathered at the Atlas Oyster House for the Independent News' April Fools' party. We hosted the event for those under forty to mingle, network, and sign up for the newly formed Pensacola Young Professionals.

Much of the discussion centered on the Pensacola City Council's vote and the anticipated benefits of the approved Community Maritime Park. Many talked about friends who had moved away because of the lack of jobs. Others admitted that they seriously considered moving to Atlanta, Orlando, or Austin if the project wasn't built.

At 7 p.m., the crowd gathered around the restaurant's televisions to watch two of their peers, John Hosman and A.J. Davis, discuss the Community Maritime Park with Fairchild and Donovan on WSRE-TV's

"Connecting the Community." The crowd cheered for the PYP leaders as they argued the group's positions in favor of the park. Some tried unsuccessfully to call into the show on their cellphones. PYP was fired up.

Fetterman Museum

The CMPA board, now just Quint and Cavanaugh, wanted the Pensacola City Council to adopt a resolution asking the Florida Legislature to approve the naming of the proposed Florida Maritime Museum in Jack's honor. State Rep. Holly Benson agreed to sponsor the legislation.

Quint said, "We have received a lot of feedback from across the state and around America on honoring him at the waterfront park he worked so hard to create."

The Pensacola City Council passed the resolution on April 13. Twelve days later, the Florida House passed a bill naming the proposed maritime museum the Vice Admiral John H. Fetterman State of Florida Maritime Museum and Research and designating it as the official state maritime museum.

Open House Party

The CMPA announced it would host an Open House Party on Saturday, April 22, from noon to 5 p.m. The party would have live music, food, a children's play area, and guided site tours. Computer-generated modeling would show the park's progression.

Ads in the News Journal and Independent News touted:

"Picture yourself strolling at sunset along the waterfront, with inviting lights, laughter, and music coming from shops and restaurants nearby as Pensacola Bay shimmers…enjoying an atmosphere Pensacola families have dreamed of, a waterfront setting that will attract local families and visitors…

Imagine all of these possibilities and so much more at Pensacola's Community Maritime Park."

"Quint wanted people to see the property, so it wasn't as scary," Jeff said. "We would have jump houses for kids, provide hot dogs and hamburgers, and give people tours of the site."

Save Our City objected to the party, accusing the city of endangering the health of those attending. Donovan emailed the city manager, saying that the Florida Department of Environmental Protection had required three feet of dirt to be placed on the site before the city could open it for human contact. "Contact with the surface soils of this site is simply not safe until the environmental remediation work is complete."

Bonfield said the issue was overblown because the entire site wasn't contaminated. The event would not be in areas cited by the state.

"Precautions have and will be taken to protect the health and well-being of any visitors participating in this event."

Though the city manager had the correct facts, Donovan had spent more than a decade building credibility with the local environmentalists. His claims discouraged some from attending the open house.

The dispute over the open house set the tone for the coming weeks. Pensacola residents had to decide which leaders to believe.

Chapter 19:
Save Our City

April 2006

For a town seeking to improve, Councilman Marty Donovan was a charismatic, stubborn, and uncompromising leader who won supporters because he was unafraid to challenge the city's power structure.

He sought to return Pensacola to its prominence in simpler times. When the Pensacola Area Chamber of Commerce asked the UWF Whitman Center for Public Service to produce a Quality of Life and Livability study, the researchers found nearly 40 percent of respondents wanted no growth in Escambia County. Forty-seven percent believed environmental quality would worsen in the next five years. Donovan embraced both those sentiments, which helped him build a following.

The councilman grew up in Pensacola and played on the Pensacola Catholic High football team with Mort O'Sullivan. His parents worked for Baars Realty for fifteen years. His dad, former Marine aviator John Donovan, sold real estate, and his mom was the office manager. In 1976, John Donovan formed Donovan Realty. Marty joined the company after spending five years in real estate appraisal. At one point, Donovan Realty had fifteen associates.

An avid fisherman, Marty chaired the Bayou Texar Foundation. He served on the City of Pensacola Citizens' Committee for Bayou Texar/Carpenters Creek Storm Water Assessment and the Escambia County Citizens' Task Force on Urban Storm Water Runoff.

Bayou Texar had suffered for decades as motor oils, pesticides, and animal waste from over sixty city drainage pipes flowed into the inlet that feeds Escambia Bay. In 1998, Donovan took over the Bayou Texar Foundation and held meetings to organize residents and pressure local and state officials to clean up the bayou. Under his leadership, it grew to more than a hundred members.

When the Florida Department of Transportation wanted to replace the Cervantes Street bridge over the Bayou Texar, Donovan criticized Bonfield for rushing to study the bridge's environmental impact to avoid construction delays.

In 2001, Donovan filed to run for the Pensacola City Council seat held by attorney John Panyko. Water pollution became his campaign issue. He accused the council of only paying lip service to remediating Bayou Texar. Donovan also wanted to scale back or abandon building a new Bayfront Auditorium and advocated selling the Trillium site. "We should not be in the real estate development business."

He defeated Panyko with 54 percent of the vote in District 4. Donovan said, "I think a lot of good people and a lot of my good friends and neighbors came together and got behind my campaign. Until we take care of our environmental problems, we can't have a strong economy."

By 2006, few people inside the city government or in the community openly challenged Donovan's statements or actions. If they disagreed, they kept their opinions to themselves.

SaveOurCityPAC.org

SaveOurCityPAC.org was blunt and used the slogans, "Stop Pensacola's Wasteful and Irresponsible Spending" and "Maritime Park Project Stinks." It described Save Our City as a "grassroots Political Action Committee (PAC), formed by concerned citizens to provide Pensacola taxpayers with a full explanation regarding the proposed construction of a baseball stadium, conference center, archaeological research center, maritime museum, and public park on the City of Pensacola-owned Trillium property."

It reiterated many of the points Fairchild, Donovan, and others had made in viewpoints and letters to the editor for months:

- The property was "very valuable and desired waterfront property."
- The city has more important needs than building a baseball stadium project that would cost taxpayers at least $80 million over the next thirty years.
- The UWF Haas Center's economic impact study was flawed.

- The CRA's mission is to eliminate slums and blight, not build baseball parks.

Its "Frequently Asked Questions" page was loaded with half-truths and misstatements. Save Our City claimed that it was formed when they became concerned about the "Pensacola City Council's poorly thought-out decision to give away valuable city-owned waterfront property worth an estimated $30,000,000 to $60,000,000, plus giving the promoters about $80,000,000 of taxpayer money to play with."

They attacked the City Council and the CMPA for not doing the "honorable thing and voluntarily allowing the citizens to decide the future of the waterfront," which they interpreted as having a referendum without requiring a petition drive. They also accused Studer and the Pensacola Chamber of intimidating the City Council and other community leaders.

Save Our City attacked Quint for not living in the city and referred to him, Jack, and Cavanaugh as a "syndicate" and a "consortium." They went after the character of all three leaders:

"One person receives a taxpayer-built baseball stadium for his baseball team and the prospect of reducing the financial losses the team has and is experiencing. He also receives a handy conference center across the street from his office, where he can hold monthly conferences for his company. Another syndicate member gets a namesake facility. The third member gets to build a larger university as a stepping stone to a job at an even larger university. These may not be bad outcomes, but it should not come on the backs of the taxpayers of Pensacola."

People could download the petition and were told to contact their city council representatives, county commissioners, and ECUA board members. The public was invited to their Tuesday meetings and asked to watch their Blab-TV program on Sunday evenings.

Donovan and Fairchild successfully recruited respected business leaders to write viewpoints for the daily newspaper. The battle of the Trillium referendum had been fought and won primarily on the News Journal's editorial pages. Save Our City wanted to follow the same political strategy against the Community Maritime Park.

In an April viewpoint in the News Journal, retired banker E.W. Hopkins wrote that the Pensacola City Council should voluntarily conduct a vote-by-mail referendum. He argued that voter turnout in voting by mail for one-issue elections in 2001 and 2003 was higher than in recent municipal elections.

He wrote, "Give the people the opportunity to vote the Maritime Park up or down."

However, not all Pensacola retirees opposed the park. A week later, former shipping executive Ted Nickinson Jr. called the referendum "a stalling tactic." In a viewpoint, he wrote, "My understanding of the American political system is that we do not submit every issue to a referendum of the voters, but that we elect representatives who then govern for limited terms in office, using their best judgment on the issues that come before them."

PNJ Editorial Battle

Columnist Mark O'Brien told PNJ readers they should sign the petition. He said the park's "liberal-style elements" ran counter to those who favor less government, lower taxes, and more personal responsibility. The park would compete for recreation dollars with movie theaters, restaurants, and bowling alleys.

O'Brien was fine with the waterfront remaining idle, at least until the Main Street Sewage Treatment Plant was relocated, which he predicted would take a minimum of four years. He called the proposed park the biggest financial decision in the city's history. The citizens should have a say because they will be liable if it flops.

PNJ Opinion editor Carl Wernicke criticized O'Brien's logic in the Sunday edition. He pointed out that the park's proponents were among the most conservative leaders in the community. The editor noted that the city's tennis courts, gyms, golf course, youth sports fields, and swimming pools already compete with the private sector.

Wernicke argued that a sense of urgency would be a welcome change from the past twenty-eight years of nothing. The sewage plant would be moved, and the maritime park's construction should take place while ECUA demolishes it.

Wernicke and Nickinson made solid points, but most voters saw little harm in allowing the public to decide the project's fate at the ballot box. Gathering petition signatures would not prove difficult.

Chapter 20:
Another Loss

May 2006

Save Our City hosted a "Turn in Your Petition" gathering at Seville Square in the Historic District on Saturday, May 13. They urged supporters to bring the petitions they had collected.

"We need to know how many more we need to meet a goal that will be comfortable and secure," Save Our City leaders wrote on their website. "We have less than two weeks to close this thing out. We need to know what areas of the city we need to do a blitz on. We must know the people who have already signed so that we do not duplicate our end-of-campaign efforts."

At the event, the PAC collected more than three hundred signatures. Donovan told the daily newspaper they had collected more than enough signatures and hoped to obtain 8,000 by the May 26 deadline. He wanted the referendum vote in July or August.

Thanks to Jeff attending their Tuesday meetings, we preempted Donovan's announcement by reporting in our May 10 issue that he had informed his followers earlier in the week that Save Our City had the signatures to force the referendum.

Once Supervisor of Elections David Stafford validated that the petition signatures met the minimum requirement, the next big decision would be whether the vote would be conducted with mail-in ballots, as it was in 2003, or in person at the polling places. Stafford would also set the date of the referendum vote.

While I didn't know which voting method was best for the park proponents, Donovan said at the May 9 meeting that he didn't think it mattered. He believed Save Our City would win regardless of the method.

I wrote, "The timing of the election is critical for Stafford's office, which needs to prepare for the fall primary. He will be pushing to do the vote as soon as legally possible."

I predicted, "Regardless of the decisions made, it looks like it will be an exciting summer with plenty to talk about and plenty of political manure to shovel through as the referendum vote approaches. You can expect the rhetoric, accusations, and conspiracy theories from Save Our City to magnify with each passing day."

Whibbs Replaces Fetterman

In mid-May, the Florida Maritime Heritage Foundation announced that it had chosen Mayor Emeritus Vince Whibbs to succeed Jack on the Community Maritime Park Associates board. The development agreement stipulated that the project would be overseen by a twelve-member board of trustees, including one representative each from the maritime foundation, Studer Group, and UWF. The City Council would appoint three members, while the CMPA would select the remaining six.

Quint told the PNJ, "Vince Whibbs, like all of us, is committed to taking Adm. Fetterman's vision to reality, to create unobstructed access to the water, a place to learn of Pensacola's great heritage through education, and a place for families to enjoy and people to learn and earn."

Oriskany

On Wednesday, May 17, a Navy demolition team sank the Oriskany 24 miles southeast of Pensacola, fulfilling Fetterman's dream of creating the world's largest artificial reef. After state and federal agencies declared it safe, the divers were allowed to enjoy the reef starting at noon on Friday.

Door-to-Door

We heard complaints about Save Our City's tactics as they gathered signatures through neighborhoods. In a letter to the editor, a reader accused the park opponents of doing a "good job of misrepresenting, distorting, and scaring many." When they knocked on his door, Save Our City volunteers said the project would raise his taxes.

"Sounds like a darn good reason to sign—if only it were true," he wrote. "Not hard to get a few thousand petition signatures this way."

He wanted Save Our City to pay for the cost of the referendum vote. "A few years from now, when this exciting park comes to life, this group will have a clear reminder of how much they cost this city back in 2006 and how very much they nearly cost us all."

Pensacola resident Evan Johns wrote he was proud of Save Our City for knocking on doors and bringing "the truth and good news to the people." He explained, "What is the good news? Well, contrary to what you heard in a pre-recorded phone message, we are allowed to challenge decisions by the City Council and, by working incredibly hard, can force the council to go forward with a referendum."

While Save Our City gathered signatures, Jeff and pro-park volunteers walked the city streets, too.

"We did it by city council district because we wanted to know within the districts where we struggled," Jeff recalled. "The park did the worst in Marty's District 4, which was East Hill and Cordova Park. We were strongest in Districts 2, 3, and 7."

Jeff kept an Excel spreadsheet with notes on every residence. "If we didn't get a contact, we'd go back. Every Saturday, we had people come out—engineers, lawyers, stay-at-home moms with kids. We had T-shirts for everybody. We'd meet up and send everyone out, saying, 'Look, do not get into heated discussions with anyone. Nobody's bad; they may not like the idea. Note it and ask what features they don't like.' And we had our list for when we'd get back together."

Friends of the Waterfront Park sent out a recorded telephone call featuring Whibbs, who urged Pensacola voters not to sign the Save Our City petitions and instead trust their elected leaders' decision on the maritime park project. This outreach prompted a viewpoint questioning how anyone could reasonably oppose citizens exercising their charter-given right to collect signatures for a referendum on such a consequential public decision.

Save Our City members suggested that representative government should be viewed merely as a practical alternative to direct democracy, chosen for convenience rather than any inherent superiority. They argued that special interests and city staff wielded excessive influence over council decisions, while individual voters could more freely express their true opinions through private ballot voting.

Presenting the Petitions

On May 24, Save Our City wanted to create a media sensation by presenting the 9,136 signed petitions at City Hall, as Donovan, Fairchild, and others opposing the Trillium project did in 2003. However, City Hall still hadn't recovered from Hurricane Ivan and reopened. The park opponents had to parade to Fire Station 1 on Cervantes Street, the temporary office for City Clerk Ericka Burnett. About twenty-five people marched the two miles from Granada Park in East Hill to the Fire Station and turned over two boxes of petitions they carried in a red wagon.

The City Charter outlined the next steps. At a public meeting, the three-member canvassing board, consisting of City Clerk Burnett, Mayor Fogg, and City Attorney John Fleming, counts the petitions and then turns them over to the Supervisor of Elections' office to verify the signatures. If the valid signatures meet the required threshold, the canvassing board notifies the Pensacola City Council, which must pass an ordinance approving the ballot language. The City Council votes on whether the referendum will be conducted by mail or at polling places.

The referendum would be held sixty days after the verification of the signatures. Most likely, the vote would happen in late July or August.

Columnist Mark O'Brien saw the petition drive's success as a "comeuppance" for park supporters, chastising them for announcing their plans in January 2005 only to have to cut amenities ten months later. The columnist failed to mention how Hurricane Katrina impacted construction costs.

O'Brien also mocked the Pensacola Young Professionals, noting several worked for Studer or O'Sullivan. He declared the "geezers" and "gray hairs" would determine the winner. O'Brien didn't write about the Black community being a factor.

Whibbs Passes

On Tuesday, May 30, Vince Whibbs collapsed in his kitchen and later died at Sacred Heart Hospital. He was headed to a television appearance to promote the Community Maritime Park.

His son, Mark Whibbs, said, "He was all dressed up and ready to speak on its behalf. He loved this city, and he became a big part of it from the moment he moved here. And he never stopped."

Vince Whibbs moved to Pensacola from Valdosta, Georgia, in 1956. He re-established the Pontiac dealership that Mort's grandfather had started and relocated it to Warrington, close to NAS Pensacola. He was elected to the Pensacola City Council in 1963 and served for two years. In 1978, Whibbs was appointed mayor and served until June 1991.

Longtime friend and golf partner Judge Lacey Collier called Whibbs "Pensacola's ambassador to the world."

Nancy Fetterman shared with the daily newspaper that Vince and Anna Whibbs had been their community sponsors who "showered them with their legendary hospitality and personal friendship" when the Fettermans arrived in Pensacola in 1991.

"My dear Jack loved Vince as a brother and knew him to be a man of character, integrity, and honor," Nancy said. "Pensacola has lost a noble man."

When Mort called him about Whibbs' death, Quint said it knocked the wind out of him. Their team had lost two inspirational leaders in two months.

"I didn't know him well before the Community Maritime Park," Quint told me later. "When I was president of Baptist Hospital, I just focused on the hospital; then, I traveled for Studer Group. So, I really didn't know Vince until Jack introduced me."

Quint said Jack and Vince would call him often and put him on speakerphone. "They knew how emotionally immature I am and how we were getting struck during the fight for the maritime park. These guys both had been there through the ups and downs of life. They had way thicker skin than overly sensitive me, and they could tell that I was struggling with my emotions. Jack and Vince would call me and lecture me—calm down, don't react, keep your powder dry."

He added, "Vince has a rare skillset. Very few people have this skill set. He could look at his role in the city critically. He truly believed that the city had to get better. And sometimes, when you have people in his role, and they've had a lot to do with the city, they get rather defensive, and they have a rough time looking in the mirror. Vince was great about saying, 'Hey, he wished he would've done this.' He saw the park as a chance for him to have an impact still."

Jeff shared with me the speech that he helped Whibbs write for his television appearance. It opened with:

157

"Who are we? What are we? If we don't know, how in the world will we ever be able to convince John Q. Pensacolian that the Community Maritime Park is the best and the only solution to the renaissance of Downtown Pensacola?

I can't answer for you, but this is what I am convinced of and who we are. We are a group of men with the vision to bring solid, sound beautification to our community through a redefinition of the highest and best use of our waterfront assets and a renaissance of pride and confidence in our community."

In closing, Whibbs planned to say that the maritime park would never happen "unless we, individually and collectively, feel and reflect the passion that we must have to convince our fellow citizens that the park is not only possible but necessary, and we can make it happen."

After his funeral, I wrote, "The passing of Vince Whibbs, the mayor emeritus of Pensacola, is another tough blow for this community. All of us who considered Vince a friend will miss his enthusiasm and zest for life."

I continued, "The question is, who will fill the leadership void left by him and Adm. Jack Fetterman? Sadly, this community has become so dependent on two 70+-year-olds to be its leaders."

The loss of the flamboyant, popular Whibbs dealt another blow to those backing the Community Maritime Park. The fight for the park would have to shift from one or two popular advocates to many less familiar faces.

Chapter 21:
A Blog is Born

June 2006

While the Supervisor of Elections validated the petition signatures, the debate over the maritime park continued to be waged in viewpoints and letters to the editors in the local papers.

An Independent News reader wrote that he had attended a few Save Our City meetings and almost succumbed to the misinformation being put forth. "Some convince me of its members that not even Jesus Christ could satisfy some of these people."

His research led him to conclude that the park would be a significant economic boost to Pensacola. "In fact, I think that the entire redevelopment of downtown Pensacola depends on the park and maritime museum being built. Not only does this affect downtown Pensacola, but the entire Pensacola Bay area's economy. We need a shining showcase to help lure business here."

In the News Journal, retired executive Bill Smart, who contributed to Save Our City, argued that eliminating the Main Street Treatment Plant should be the top priority. He didn't want Pensacola to take on any major project until all the funding for its demolition and relocation was guaranteed and secured. He described the stadium as a limited-use ballpark that would sit vacant for three hundred days annually.

Smart refused to believe any other events would be held in the stadium. He questioned why UWF would want a downtown building when it had 600 acres of unused land on its main campus. He liked the maritime museum but thought the Trillium site limited its ability to expand. He recommended delaying any project for two years.

How to Blog

In June, my editor, Duwayne Escobedo, and I jumped in my 1997 Jeep Cherokee, drove ten hours overnight, and rolled into Little Rock, Arkansas, around sunrise for the annual convention of the Association of Alternative Newsweeklies. We weren't there to escape Pensacola—we sought membership not only to benchmark our publication but also to help fight Gannett, owner of the Pensacola News Journal.

AAN had rejected our two previous applications. In 2002, the membership committee found Joe Scarborough's involvement and political agenda too much to swallow, calling our paper "weirdly right-wing." After he quit Congress and our weekly, we tried again in 2004, but AAN took offense at my being on the Gulf Breeze City Council and compared our news and features to Fox News.

Duwayne and I felt our reporting since Hurricane Ivan gave us our best chance yet, so we tried again in 2006. The convention speakers included former President Bill Clinton, retired General Wesley Clark, and Susan McDougal, who spent twenty-two months in jail for refusing to answer Prosecutor Kenneth Starr's questions before a grand jury about her partnership with the Clintons on the Whitewater development.

At the Historic Arkansas Museum's fish fry, I met Arkansas Times editor Max Brantley. Over beers, we discussed his blog because I had attended his panel discussion earlier in the day and wanted to figure out how to utilize the tool.

I learned how blogs had evolved since 1994, starting as online journals with daily entries about mundane activities. By 2006, platforms like Blogger, WordPress, and LiveJournal had made blogging more mainstream. Alternative weeklies were using blogs to break into daily news coverage.

"A blog is a way for weeklies to become dailies," Brantley told me. "It pushes the boundaries of interactivity. You must have fresh content constantly."

As dusk turned to night, we moved to a nearby dive bar. I wanted to know the secret to making a blog have an impact. I created a WordPress blog in 2005, but it didn't get much attention. I rarely posted anything, writing only once or twice a month; I wasn't sure how to use it.

"Rick, you have to post three times a day, every day. Post everything you hear, read, or that someone sends you. Eventually, you will break a big news story that no one else has, and readers will flock to you," Brantley said. He emphasized timing, recommending posts before 8 a.m., around 11 a.m., and after 5 p.m.

The next morning, we received another rejection. The AAN judges wrote, "You've got to admire owner-publisher Rick Outzen's enterprise and editorial output. He's all over this paper—in the promising news section, anyway—boosting a local business one minute, bashing Bush the next. He's also on a local city council but says he's stepping down in November."

They added, "He can't do it all, and the paper suffers for not having other competent contributors. The arts coverage is universally tepid... If the paper can't add staffers, then it needs to hire more good freelancers to develop a more local voice instead of New York Times South."

Their final assessment stung: "This paper has its eye on the ball, but some editorial choices lead to excessive head-scratching."

Duwayne and I packed our bags. Instead of lamenting the rejection, we discussed how I would change my blog. Whizzing down Interstate 55 at 7 a.m., we pulled off at Como, Miss., to swing by my alma mater, the University of Mississippi. At Ole Miss, I showed Duwayne the bullet holes in the Lyceum columns from 1962, when the National Guard protected James Meredith as he integrated the university.

Behind it was the library, which had once housed the post office where William Faulkner worked, and he was reportedly terrible at his job. When asked later about his postal experience, Faulkner said, "Thank God I won't ever again have to be at the beck and call of every son of a bitch who's got two cents to buy a stamp."

The camaraderie and laughter were good for our souls as we braced for the Community Maritime Park battle.

Rick's Blog 2.0

I immediately implemented Brantley's recommendations, posting more times in June than in all of 2005. I used the blog to counter the Save Our City viewpoints and letters in the daily newspaper.

Elebash and other anti-park advocates liked to use the book "Sports, Jobs & Taxes: Are New Stadiums Worth the Cost?" to validate their position that the CRA shouldn't build a stadium.

I pointed out that the study was based on data from a decade ago and was concerned with Major League Baseball parks and NFL stadiums. The economics for minor league ballparks in downtown areas were completely different, especially because of the financial commitments Quint pledged toward the project. I listed fourteen differences on the blog.

"If you truly want to do an independent, scientific analysis of the CMP and the baseball park then you have to compare apples to apples,"

I wrote. "The Brookings study isn't applicable to the CMP proposal any more than 'The Da Vinci Code' is to Catholicism.

I followed with another post pointing out that the book only had one chapter devoted to minor league ballparks. The three parks studied cost considerably more and had double the capacity of the proposed Pensacola multi-use stadium. The most successful of the trio was the Mercer County Waterfront Park, built in downtown Trenton, New Jersey, for one of the best franchises in the minors.

I also responded to Bill Smart's viewpoint that Pensacola should not take on many major projects until funding is secured to eliminate the sewage treatment plant. I noted that ECUA owns, operates, and receives all revenue from the current plant and any future plants. ECUA will not repay the city for any contribution to move the facility.

"The financial responsibility for relocating the Main Street Sewage Treatment Plant falls on ECUA, not the City or Escambia County,' I wrote. "Save Our City is upset that the Pensacola Pelicans may make money off the new baseball park but isn't upset the ECUA will make millions off the new plant and not share any of it with the city."

A reader commented that he was upset that Quint wouldn't commit to sharing with the City of Pensacola any profit made from the future sale of the Pensacola Pelicans.

"What is the crime in Quint someday selling the Pensacola Pelicans for a profit? Did Charlie Fairchild, the Save Our City founder, give the city a share of the profit from selling his office building on South Palafox, which benefited from all the work the CRA has done downtown? No, of course not. None of us is expected to do so," I replied.

"Does the federal government expect the scuba businesses whose value has increased due to the sinking of the Oriskany to share any profits from the sale of the business (beyond taxes, of course)? No," I wrote. "When ECUA moves the Main Street Sewage Treatment Plant, will every home and business owner in the city be expected to give any profit they make from selling their homes or businesses to ECUA? No."

I continued, "The businesses near the airport benefit from any improvements to the airport. Will they share their profits when they're sold with the city? No. Such things only happen in socialist or communist countries."

I did more than write on the blog about Save Our City and the Community Maritime Park. The blog reported on various statewide primaries, the national midterm elections, the latest jail deaths, the AAN convention, Martini Night conversations, my difficulties getting public records, and the Santa Rosa County Republican Party's executive committee opposing a penny local sales tax for roads.

State Honors Fetterman

On Thursday, June 22, Gov. Jeb Bush signed the bill making Pensacola's proposed museum the official state maritime museum, named the "Vice Admiral John H. Fetterman State of Florida Museum and Research Center."

Nancy Fetterman traveled to Tallahassee to sign the bill. She said, "He was the frontman for the museum. It became a mission for him. He felt like the community needed something like this."

At the ceremony, Gov. Bush said, "Nancy, you know your husband was an incredible patriot and a great public servant. He served our nation with honor and distinction, and this museum pays him a fitting tribute."

Save Our City made no mention of the ceremony but directed more of its criticism toward Quint Studer and the multi-use stadium.

Petitions Validated

The process for scheduling the referendum moved forward when David Stafford, the Supervisor of Elections, confirmed 7,122 valid petition signatures and officially presented his findings to the city canvassing on June 20. After the board's acceptance, the matter proceeded to the Pensacola City Council, where the ballot ordinance would take two public hearings.

The council held its first reading on June 22, with the second reading scheduled for July 13. Given the timeline, Stafford indicated September 5 as the most feasible date for the referendum, coinciding with the statewide primary elections. He explained that conducting a separate election earlier wasn't practical due to the primary's early voting requirements and military overseas ballot logistics.

While Donovan expressed frustration that the period between signature verification and the vote was twenty-four days longer than the charter mandated, he ultimately accepted the timing constraint. The council unanimously approved the September 5 date.

Having the referendum as part of the primary pleased Jeff DeWeese because the election would not cost Pensacola citizens anything. He said, "Let's go on and settle this issue once and for all."

Chapter 22:
Smoking Gun

June 2006

Save Our City seized the media spotlight by holding a press conference on the steps of Pensacola City Hall, just fifteen minutes before the Pensacola City Council met on June 23. Charlie Fairchild distributed ten pages of emails that he alleged demonstrated a conspiracy between Quint Studer, UWF President John Cavanaugh, and others to restrict public input on maritime park plans and manipulate the City Council.

"Over the past year and one half, we have become increasingly concerned about the seemingly irrational direction the Trillium Maritime project has been taking from the illogical, nearly unanimous support of the Pensacola City Council to the operations of the 'public' meetings to the unusual delays for no apparent reason in the Trillium 2 referendum vote," Fairchild said.

The emails had been in Save Our City's possession for almost a year, obtained through a public record request from Cavanaugh and City Manager Tom Bonfield the previous summer. According to Fairchild, these emails provided evidence for their conspiracy claims.

"We believe the time has come to take a hard look at exactly who is pushing this project and exactly what role the city staff and City Council have had and continue to play in the manipulation of the public in this matter," he told reporters.

"We anticipate that more telling information will be forthcoming in the near future, which will reveal this project was orchestrated from the beginning to deprive the citizens of their waterfront property so that a baseball stadium and a UWF waterfront campus could be built on the Trillium property."

Damning Emails?

After reviewing the documents Fairchild had distributed, I shared what he considered the most incriminating emails on my blog, along with my analysis.

The first significant exchange he highlighted was from November 2004, involving Mike Thiessen (Quint's baseball consultant for stadium financing), architect Miller Caldwell, and Bonfield. The emails discussed finding an alternative to the American Creosote site for the ballpark. Thiessen had expressed concerns after meeting with EPA officials, and the city manager wanted Quint to consult with urban planner Ray Gindroz.

While Fairchild claimed these emails showed a conspiracy between Studer's team and Bonfield, I pointed out on my blog that he had

170

overlooked crucial context from the same exchange. Caldwell had explicitly confirmed the EPA's stance against using the American Creosote Site for construction, noting, "The Corps of Engineers has more testing to get a better handle on the amount of contaminated material to be moved and stored on-site, which they estimate may take three to four months."

Bonfield's response had been pragmatic: "I am doubtful that we are going to have many answers even by then. It may be time to consider moving on to alternate sites. Let me know when we can discuss this."

I emphasized in my analysis that developers routinely met with city staff before presenting commercial and residential projects to the City Council. "It makes good business sense to do so; thereby, it saves time and costs and ensures the project meets city and county codes. No crime was committed there."

The next set of emails Fairchild distributed involved a January 2005 exchange between Quint's attorney, Bob Hart, and city staff regarding potential bond issues. The discussions revealed that CRA funds could potentially support $29 million to $40 million in bonds. Fairchild accused Bonfield of circumventing the City Council's Strategic Plan 2003-2009, which called for community involvement in Trillium/Bruce Beach area planning.

"The next thing we know, the Trillium site is the site for the project," Fairchild declared. "The council has had private meetings with the promoters, and approval is given for the project."

I countered this interpretation on my blog: "Again, no laws are broken. To explore whether the waterfront park could or should be a public/private venture, both sides needed to see what options were available."

The most contentious emails Fairchild shared involved E.W. Bullock Associates. After the Committee of the Whole presentation on January 15, 2005, Ellis Bullock wrote enthusiastically: "In the 15+ years I have worked with the City of Pensacola, I have never witnessed anything like I did this afternoon. Each of you did an outstanding job. I believe you left all council members and staff in a state of shock, each not sure what to make of the matter because they've never experienced anything like it."

Bullock employee Raad Cawthon's subsequent email became a focal point of controversy, particularly his statement: "We have at least five votes in our pocket (Fogg, Wiggins, Nobles, DeSorbo, and Wu)."

He also wrote, "At this point, if we stay ahead of the game, I do not think there is anything for the opposition to coalesce around. Staff will look at this proposal, but Bonfield has a strong sense of where this is going."

When I contacted Ellis Bullock about these emails, he clarified that Community Maritime Park Associates never paid his firm, and they had ceased working with the park proponents after their January 2005 council appearance.

I addressed the controversy on my blog, noting that Cawthon's writing "in our pocket" was "a poor choice of words." I concluded: "But no one takes seriously that they meant the five were paid off in any way. If so, then Save Our City needs more proof. We must also remember that Save Our City is picking and choosing the emails it shows us. They are not releasing anything that works against their position."

The blog discussion of the press conference and the emails became the viral moment that Max Brantley predicted would happen if I consistently posted on the blog.

Readers Comment

A seismic shift occurred on Rick's Blog. The steady trickle of readers I'd grown accustomed to suddenly became a deluge. The email controversy ignited a firestorm, but not the one Fairchild expected.

The comments section erupted almost immediately. "So Quint Stupid (sic) and a few of his cronies get rich off this thing. What's wrong with that?" wrote one critic.

But before I could respond, another reader jumped to the defense: "Read the lease and development agreements. Then tell me how Studer is getting rich from this plan. If Jesus Christ performed the miracle of the Loaves and Fishes in Pensacola, some would complain the fish wasn't fried."

The biblical reference drew swift fire: "Well, if you think the CMP is akin to the miracle of loaves & fishes, please carry on. You are deluded beyond help."

What followed was a days-long battle in the comments, with readers returning obsessively to witness each new salvo. The park's defenders mounted a methodical campaign, outlining taxpayer protections embedded in the agreements, systematically dismantling accusations about Quint's motives, and arguing that the benefits far outweighed any risks. They pressed Save Our City to reveal their alternative vision should the referendum fail.

The opposition stuck to their familiar refrains, recycling concerns about leasing land for a dollar, questioning the return on investment, raising the alarm about hurricane risks, and challenging the bidding process. I stepped back, letting readers navigate the crossfire and draw their conclusions.

Chapter 23:
Trading Punches

July 2006

The press conference was only the first of many punches Save Our City delivered as the summer of 2006 began to heat up.

Fairchild sent a letter to Mayor John Fogg demanding Save Our City's inclusion in any presentations, literature, mailouts, letters, or other communications concerning the Community Maritime Park that used city resources. He also wanted the city to give his group equal time in approximately the same time slot on any radio or television station.

They requested that all communications from the city manager, city employees, and council members regarding the referendum include the following statement:

"A petition drive by voters in Pensacola has forced the city to hold a referendum on the Project. Their information and position can be found at WWW.SaveOurCityPAC.org or Phone 221-3839."

Fairchild aimed to portray the city as the enemy of the people. He wanted voters to distrust both the town and any materials coming from it. The letter reinforced Save Our City's conspiracy allegations, while city officials viewed the request as an overreach and chose to ignore it.

Luke McCoy

Besides Mark O'Brien, Save Our City had another powerful media personality in its corner.

Luke McCoy was a significant media voice in Pensacola as the host of WCOA's "Pensacola Speaks" call-in show and morning news program with Don Parker. Since 1993, he had built a loyal following among listeners who tuned in for his conservative commentary on local politics and his platform for citizens to voice their grievances about local government and media.

McCoy, whose real name was Luther Ralton Eason, had deep roots in Pensacola. He moved there in 1956 and graduated from Pensacola High School in 1957. His military service included time with both the U.S. Army's 82nd Airborne Division and the U.S. Marine Corps, where he served in Vietnam and earned a Purple Heart. His military background remained evident in his show, where he often exchanged the Marine greeting "Semper Fi" with callers.

WCOA marketed him as "the common man's intellectual," and his show flourished alongside conservative syndicated hosts like Rush Limbaugh, Glenn Beck, and Sean Hannity. His conservative stances resonated with listeners, particularly his advocacy for traditional values, exemplified by his promotion of phrases like "Merry Christmas with extra Jesus."

In May 2006, McCoy launched WASPO (We Are Seriously Pissed Off) out of his frustration with the lack of border enforcement. He believed President George W. Bush was not doing enough to stop the influx of illegal migrants from Mexico. McCoy created a WASPO button, a WASPO Pensacola Nest membership card, and a website to support his cause.

The movement gained quick traction, with over a hundred people attending a WASPO luncheon at Mesquite Charlie's, a cowboy-themed steakhouse on North W Street. O'Brien helped popularize WASPO through his column. McCoy explained to O'Brien that he created WASPO because he believed illegal migrants were "destroying what I have always known as America."

McCoy's influence extended to local development issues. He strongly opposed both the 2003 Trillium Plan and the Community Maritime Park proposal, frequently providing airtime to Donovan and Fairchild. This bias became evident when, in early July, Q100 Morning crew host John Stuart filled in on "Pensacola Speaks" during McCoy's vacation. Stuart's challenge to the anti-park perspective angered Donovan so much that he demanded WCOA remove Stuart from the air—a request the station denied.

For the Independent News, McCoy represented those who opposed change. I enjoyed the challenge of seeing if our little newspaper could beat him on a political issue. We loved to provoke him whenever possible. The rivalry between McCoy's show and the Independent News added another layer of intrigue to Pensacola's political landscape.

Baseball Challenge Refused

C.C. Elebash faced criticism from his Save Our City colleagues for not accepting my challenge to analyze minor league baseball teams with ballparks built in downtown areas over the past ten years. I proposed reviewing baseball teams in Charleston, South Carolina; Chattanooga, Tennessee; Fort Worth, Texas; Greenville, South Carolina; Louisville, Kentucky; and Montgomery, Alabama.

The retired college professor said it couldn't be done because only one city had a similar population size. In an email to Save Our City followers, Elebash wrote, "All the cities have larger populations than Pensacola, except for Greenville. All the teams have minor league status except for Pensacola and Fort Worth. These two are in an 'independent' league. Pensacola is definitely not comparable to Fort Worth because the latter is in a large metropolitan area."

He criticized independent teams, like the Pensacola Pelicans, for existing on "the fringes of baseball" because they were not affiliated with Major League Baseball (MLB) franchises. Elebash asserted that small franchises initially drew well, but public interest eventually faded. "For example, Florida State League (Single A) teams had an average attendance of about 1,300 in 2005. Pelicans' paid attendance has apparently also averaged less than 1,500."

I dissected Elebash's email on the blog, pointing out that when businesses and economists determine the Pensacola customer base, they look at the entire Metropolitan Statistical Area (MSA), which has a population of 436,210. Only Fort Worth had a higher population of 535,000.

I continued, "Using this population number, Charleston, Greenville, Chattanooga, and Montgomery are very fair comparisons, especially when considering the size of the proposed park compared to its facilities."

Elebash understated the Pelicans' average attendance, which was nearly 1,650 per game in a substandard park with few amenities in a remote location at the University of West Florida. I argued that location, not MLB affiliation, was the key to improving attendance.

I also noted that the Florida State League's attendance was less than the Pelicans average. I wrote, "I find it interesting that you're using an affiliated league to prove your point. Could it be that affiliation or independence really isn't that important after all?"

Elebash didn't reply.

CMPA Pep Rally

On Thursday, July 6, CMPA rallied to recruit volunteers to campaign door-to-door for the Community Maritime Park. More than 250 people showed up, and with the vote sixty-one days away, they picked up stickers and yard signs with the message, "I'm For the Waterfront Park. Vote Yes!"

Quint Studer, UWF President John Cavanaugh, Nancy Fetterman, and others gave rousing speeches in Seville Quarter's Heritage Hall. Elected officials, business leaders, PYP members, and park supporters filled the room.

Quint read aloud the late Vince Whibbs' speech, which the mayor emeritus intended to give before his sudden death. He then announced the pro-park campaign slogan, "Let's do it together; let's do it now."

He exhorted the crowd to help inform the public about the park's merits. "We need to let the public know that it will bring 1,500 jobs to the area, create opportunities downtown, and keep our young, talented citizens in Pensacola."

Nancy called on the City Council to name the park after Whibbs. Cavanaugh stressed the importance of connecting Pensacola's maritime heritage with the park's museum.

Tale of Two Meetings

On Tuesday, July 11, the Pensacola Young Professionals and Save Our City held organizational meetings. The contrast was stark.

At Sacred Heart Cathedral's parish hall, seventy-four Young Professionals attended a general meeting. I wrote, "They were in a wide variety of professions, shapes, and colors, and very representative of the community."

The members voted unanimously to support the Community Maritime Park and signed up to promote it door-to-door.

A mile away on Bayou Texar, Save Our City gathered at the Bayview Senior Center. According to Jeff DeWeese, who attended, the leaders focused on their political targets. They discussed the allegations that Fairchild had presented in late June, stating that Ellis Bullock and his firm had a conflict of interest in representing the city while working with Community Maritime Park Associates.

The leaders planned to make additional public record requests of Cavanaugh, Mort, Bonfield, DeWeese, Bullock, Raad Cawthon, Jane Birdwell, Downtown Improvement Board Executive Director Kim Kimbrough, CRA Director David Bailey, and Pensacola Chamber CEO Evon Emerson, even though some were private citizens, and their records were not subject to Florida's Sunshine laws.

Save Our City members evaluated potential candidates for upcoming council seats. They discussed a possible new red herring—the need to dredge Pensacola Bay near the location. The estimated cost would run into millions of dollars, funds not allocated to the current budget.

Upsetting Save Our City

Political action committees in Florida can advocate for candidates, but they must remain independent and focus primarily on issues rather than individuals. I stirred things up on the blog by suggesting that they might have violated Florida PAC regulations when they openly discussed their candidate endorsements for city elections and potential challengers to Mayor Fogg.

I later sought clarification from David Stafford, the Supervisor of Elections. According to him, while PACs could engage in candidate discussions, they were prohibited from spending resources on candidates. I explained it this way on the blog: "In other words, no Save Our City checks for candidates. Your paid staff can't do work for Marty Donovan or other candidates. You can't let them use your office on Ninth Avenue. Other than that, you should be okay."

A reader sent me an email chain between Save Our City leaders. Donovan's wife, Helene, was upset that I posted notes on what happened inside their public meetings. Blair Stephenson, who served on the Bayou

Texar Foundation with her husband, wanted Jeff kicked out of the Tuesday meetings.

Stephenson wrote Helene, "Jeff has got to go. It may be a public meeting, but just as you'd oust someone for disrupting a meeting for other reasons, we can and must oust someone who is quietly, and sometimes not quietly (his debate with Charles in the last meeting), intent on damaging us. I will volunteer to come early and deliver the message myself to Jeff."

Elebash added, "I agree with Blair that Jeff DeWeese should be 'uninvited' to the Tuesday evening meetings. He has taken advantage of our hospitality. Also, he did not invite us to his meeting where there was free food and beverages."

Gallery Night Buzz

On Friday, July 14, the Arts Council of Northwest Florida held its Summer Gallery Night to celebrate the area's artists and draw visitors to downtown Pensacola. We hosted a pirate-themed party with Mr. Margarita and served over 800 frozen margaritas.

After the party, I followed Max Brantley's formula and posted on the blog the highlights of my conversations with the nine hundred people who stopped by our office to hear Lindsey Battle sing and buy her latest CD.

Here are my notes—the train-of-thought version:

People were shocked when Marty Donovan voted against letting the public vote on the DIB expansion. Everyone thought he said the public should have the right to vote—at least, that's what he told voters to get them to sign the park petition, right?

Rumor has it that the FBI is investigating the Robert Boggan and Jerry Preyer deaths at the jail. No confirmation. Also, the accreditation for the Escambia Country Jails's infirmary is up for renewal this month. Inspectors are expected in two weeks. Do they know about the deaths? How many deaths does it take to receive demerits?

County Administrator George Touart is trying to get on the program to speak to the PYP to clear up any "misunderstandings." When I think of it, I don't believe the county has any employees in the PYP. On the other hand, the City of Pensacola does. Either the County has few employees who qualify for Pensacola Young Professionals, or they're afraid to join a group that the IN helped found. Interesting. I suggest that if the county wants to improve its relationship with young professionals, it should encourage them to join. That would go a long way.

Visitors to the Independent News remarked that "every weekend would be like if the Community Maritime Park is built." They asked where Fairchild, Donovan, Elebash, and other Save Our City leaders were and why they were not downtown businesses on Gallery Night.

One guest said, "Save Our City may be the first generation that doesn't give a damn about the younger generations. It's all about them."

A lot of positive comments on the paper, which isn't unusual, especially after a few drinks. But the remarks were encouraging. Several readers sought me out to praise my work.

Those who had read the blog wondered why Save Our City was upset about someone attending their open meetings and reporting on them. Didn't they accuse their opposition of operating behind closed doors? Shouldn't it take the high road?

We heard that the Community Maritime Park Associates will put out ads soon. No more sitting quietly on the sidelines.

Chapter 24:
For the Kids

July 2006

In our July 13 issue, my "Outtakes" stressed the importance of the Community Maritime Park to Pensacola's future:

> The Independent News has analyzed the park proposal. We are in favor of the project because we believe it will be a catalyst for revitalizing not only Pensacola but also all of Escambia County.
>
> The facts are that this area is far behind the rest of the region, the rest of the state, and the rest of the nation. Escambia is the poorest large county in Florida and the 17th poorest county in the U.S., and one out of five citizens lives below the poverty level.
>
> Our unemployment rate is low, but so are our wages. The average hourly rate in the greater Pensacola area is $13.04, while the state average is $15.30. Our biggest employers aren't private industry but local government agencies that we finance with taxes and fees.
>
> Environmentally, we're also lacking. We lead North Florida in the number of federal Superfund sites with five. Statewide, only Miami-Dade, Hillsborough, and Broward counties have more. Each of those has huge metropolitan areas and much stronger economies.

It is little wonder that the population of Escambia County is relatively flat. While the state of Florida has grown at the rate of 8.8 percent in the past four years, Escambia County has grown a measly 1.5 percent. Neighboring Baldwin County has seen its population jump 11.6 percent.

Our young people are leaving us in droves. Recent economic studies show that 11 percent of our under-35-year-olds have moved away since 2000.

Some would argue that this area is more than falling behind. It's dying.

This is why we believe the Maritime Park is so important. It can be the spark to reverse the tide.

However, it's more than that for me.

The Community Maritime Park is the best chance we have to keep our children here and not lose them to Atlanta, Orlando, or Austin. Most of those who oppose waterfront parks have already lost their children to these and other cities. Other supporters are retirees who moved here after their children had grown up. They couldn't care less about your or my children.

Me? I admit I'm selfish. I want my three daughters and their families to live here. I want them to find good-paying jobs here. I want them to be able to afford a nice home in a safe neighborhood. I want them to be so proud of this area that they would invite their friends to come live here, too.

The Community Maritime Park isn't about Quint Studer and the Pensacola Pelicans. It's not about the University of West Florida, the Pensacola City Council, Charles Fairchild, Marty Donovan, or Rick Outzen.

The Community Maritime Park is about our future, our children, and their children. I hope you will keep that in mind over the long, hot weeks that lead up to the Sept. 5 referendum.

Democrat Party Upset

Ron Melton, Escambia Democratic Party chair, objected to my "Outtakes." He saw my comment that Community Maritime Park opponents didn't care about our children as "divisive."

"Contrary to Mr. Outzen's opinion, I have found the retirees involved in the Maritime Park issue and other local issues very concerned about both the children of Pensacola and Pensacola's future," Melton wrote. "Mr. Outzen and other promoters of the proposed Maritime Park project have tried to paint themselves as progressives and those who want to vote on the project as regressive. I believe it is the other way around, and the advertising firms and promoters of this project are using double-speak."

He added, "Mr. Outzen should apologize to the retirees in our area."

I responded, "I see nothing progressive about stopping a waterfront project that will bring thousands of jobs and revitalize our community. I've not heard one member of Save Our City say we're stopping the Community Maritime Park for our grandchildren."

Marty's Emails

On July 14, I requested Councilman Donovan's e-mails concerning the Community Maritime Park. Save Our City had demanded thousands of records from Community Maritime Park supporters. We wanted to review Donovan's written communications about the park proposal to understand better how the opposition campaign developed.

I received a letter from the city clerk dated July 17 stating that the request had been passed on to Donovan to fulfill. The councilman didn't hand over his emails until August 11.

Chuckie & Donno

In mid-July, Friends of the Waterfront Park PAC released a series of animated cartoons to address Save Our City's misinformation. The ads featured two older men in late 19th-century suits sitting in stuffed chairs on the vacant Trillium site. Chuckie and Donno represented Charlie Fairchild and Marty Donovan.

Dick Appleyard came up with the idea, and his news media director, Joe Vinson, developed the ads based on Statler and Waldorf, the grumpy puppets that ended each episode of "The Muppet Show." The ads would later win the Appleyard Agency the award for Best Broadcast ad from the Pensacola chapter of the American Advertising Federation.

Appleyard recalled, "Joe thought the animated ad could be hilarious and make points that needed to be made. Nobody had ever done an animated ad in Pensacola before. Quint didn't care about cost and gave us the go-ahead."

"I was glad we played offense," Quint said. "Pensacola knew Marty was a bully and gave him a pass. Marty, Charlie, and C.C. weren't used to being challenged."

He added, "They might object, but at least they knew we weren't going just to sit there and be silent."

The first ad was titled "Stop Our City," the nickname we had given to Save Our City. It focused on correcting the misinformation that the Community Maritime Park would increase taxes.

STOP OUR CITY

Chuckie: You know, Donno, that bit about the park increasing taxes is genius.

Donno: Thanks, Chuckie. If we get the voters to think they're paying, we'll stop this park. Maybe even stop all this talk about the future.

Chuckie: Yeah. Don't let the voters find out the tax fund already exists.

Donno: Or that only businesses and homes downtown pay for it.

Chuckie: And that the business pays 75 percent.

Donno: No, sir, don't tell them the facts, they might vote for fun, for Waterfront access, for education, and the economy.

Chuckie: I'm against it, Donno.

Donno: Against what?

Chuckie: Everything. (Laughter)

The second ad, "Forever Glum," teased that Save Our City didn't care about young professionals. The punch line was, "Right when young people lose, we win." The third cartoon, "Ballpark Blitz," parodied the park opponents' efforts to make the referendum about the ballpark while ignoring the maritime museum, conference center, retail space, and green space.

The fourth one, "Dollar Diddle," mocked Save Our City's position that the city was giving away the land for a dollar. It ended with:

Dunno: That's why we dreamed up the $1 land giveaway.

Chuckie: "I'm for it, Donno.

Donno: "For what?"

Chuckie: "Nothing." (Laughter)

The ads infuriated Fairchild, Donovan, and Save Our City members.

Knocking on Doors

On Saturday, July 22, Friends of the Waterfront Park launched their neighborhood canvassing effort. Led by Jeff DeWeese and supported by political consultants Bruce Barcelo and Tom Nolan, over a hundred volunteers spread across all seven city districts.

Barcelo & Company, known for their expertise in passing tax initiatives and referendums, guided Quint's team for nearly a year. Their

192

strategy centered on positive messaging. "People naturally want to support something rather than oppose it," Jeff explained. "That was fundamental to their approach."

After visiting the Trillium site, Barcelo and Nolan recognized the challenge ahead. They emphasized the need for visual renderings and recommended positioning the project as a multi-use facility rather than just a baseball park. They also encouraged Jeff to monitor Save Our City meetings to stay informed about opposition concerns.

The campaign was meticulously organized. Barcelo provided detailed street maps showing each resident's party affiliation, helping volunteers tailor their approach. The team followed strict canvassing hours—no earlier than 9 a.m. or later than 4 p.m. on Saturdays. On Sundays, they started after 2 p.m. to respect family time.

After each weekend, Jeff reported back to Barcelo and Nolan about what the volunteers heard. "If we had people objecting in a neighborhood, the volunteer would ask if we could send them any additional information and record their name and address. Tom would mail them a package of information. It was amazing."

Weekly debriefs revealed interesting patterns. East Hill and Cordova Park showed the highest number of undecided voters, with an even split among those who had made up their minds. Other districts, particularly in Black neighborhoods, demonstrated strong support. Jeff said, "Some walkers reported fifty out of fifty-two home visits in favor of the park."

The main opposition came from residents who felt disconnected from downtown, questioning their stake in the project. Age also played a factor, with voters over seventy generally showing more resistance to the park.

The door-to-door campaign's progress was regularly documented on the blog, keeping supporters informed about the community's response.

City Tax Cut

On July 24, the Pensacola City Council's Finance Committee recommended a decrease in the city property tax rate. Under the proposal, which the City Council later approved, the rate would decrease to 4.95 mils. If approved, the change would be reflected in a property owner's 2007 tax bill. The rate had been at 5.057 mils for thirteen consecutive years.

"At a time when many citizens are still struggling with the aftermath of Hurricanes Ivan and Dennis, we think it is prudent that the City Council be sensitive to these needs and render some relief," said Finance Committee Chairman Mike DeSorbo. "We want the citizens to know we understand what they are going through."

The reduction would leave the proposed 2007 City general fund budget at $56.5 million. When I reported on the meeting on the blog, I wrote, "Looks like CRA isn't draining the city coffers after all. The rollback makes sound financial sense."

Here Comes the Judge

On July 25, Community Maritime Park Associates announced that U.S. District Judge Lacey Collier had agreed to serve on its board of directors, joining UWF President John Cavanaugh and Quint Studer. Judge Collier replaced his long-time friend, Pensacola Mayor Emeritus Vince Whibbs, who served briefly until his death in June.

"I feel honored and proud to be in the position of following in the footsteps of two very, very good friends," Collier said. "It is not overstating to say they were both legends in their service to our community.

He added, "My purpose in serving on the Community Maritime Park board is to help ensure that once we go forward, we will have a true community park designed to benefit all the citizens of the Pensacola area, as both Vince and Jack envisioned. I can do no less in honoring the memory of the two great men who went before me."

Judge Collier's distinguished career began with two decades of service in the U.S. Navy, where he achieved the rank of lieutenant commander. His military accomplishments included logging over 5,000 flight hours, completing 450 carrier landings, and flying 140 combat missions over North Vietnam.

Following his military service, Collier pursued a legal career, earning his Juris Doctor degree from Florida State University College of

Law. He served as an assistant state attorney in Florida's First Judicial Circuit from 1977 to 1984, then as a circuit judge in the same jurisdiction until 1991.

When President George H. W. Bush nominated him to a newly created seat on the United States District Court for the Northern District of Florida, Collier made history as the first Florida State University law graduate to serve on the federal bench. He transitioned to senior status in November 2003.

Perhaps Judge Collier's most enduring legacy lies in his advocacy for children with disabilities. In December 2005, the Escambia County School District honored his contributions by naming the Lacey A. Collier Snoezelen Sensory Complex at the Escambia Westgate Center after him. This facility serves approximately 240 students with severe mental and physical disabilities and represents a pioneering achievement in specialized education.

The complex, which school officials dubbed the "Sistine Chapel of Snoezelen," broke new ground as North America's first facility of its kind. It employs the Snoezelen concept, an innovative therapeutic approach that uses multisensory experiences—including carefully designed lighting, colors, shapes, textures, aromas, and music—to help children with autism and other developmental disabilities better engage with their environment and develop connections with the world around them.

Though not as vocal as his predecessors on the park board, Judge Collier was a worthy replacement for Jack and Vince and added more credibility to the Community Maritime Park project.

Chapter 25:
Momentum Shifts

August 2006

In addition to Luke McCoy on WCOA and Mark O'Brien in the News Journal, Save Our City relied on BLAB-TV to get its message before Pensacola voters.

"BLAB" (Basic Local Area Broadcasting or Basic Local Audience Broadcasting) was started by college roommates Fred Levin and Fred Vigodsky. BLAB TV debuted on February 1, 1984, with a 90-minute program and quickly expanded to 24-hour broadcasting. In 2006, it had a channel in the lower range of cable television channels, making it easily accessible.

Most of the shows were infomercials for local businesses. Still, it was also credited with launching the political career of little-known attorney Joe Scarborough, who bought time every afternoon on the channel when he successfully ran for Congress in 1994.

Our staff watched the Save Our City shows and countered their disinformation on the blog. Donovan, Fairchild, and various citizens appeared on the show. They called the park a giveaway, saying the waterfront was being leased for only a dollar a year.

I wrote, "Come on, Marty. The dollar-a-year lease is only half the story. Tell the citizens that the city gets all the sublease from the property, which must be at fair market value. Every business built on the property, including the Studer Group building, must pay a sublease fee to the City of Pensacola. It's much more than a dollar-a-year lease involved here."

They described the $40-million bond issue as a loan to Studer. I replied, "The $40 million loan doesn't go to Quint Studer. It pays for the multi-use stadium, conference center, and public park areas. Funds are released as the city approves construction invoices. The loan is paid back by the CRA funds generated from the property itself."

Since the CRA receives funds from the incremental improvement in downtown property values, the opponents protested that "$2 million was diverted out of the county general fund."

I wrote, "Why is it a bad idea for the county to help the downtown area? Most of the key county offices are located downtown and don't pay property taxes. If the county weren't paying for something, Save Our City would be whining that the City was paying for something that county residents were using."

They also called the CRA budget "a slush fund for developers from Pensacola Beach."

I responded, "Adm. Jack Fetterman wasn't a developer from Pensacola Beach. John Cavanaugh and Quint Studer aren't Pensacola

199

Beach developers. It doesn't take much for Save Our City to start name-calling."

The opponents protested that the first phase would not include "a marina and other amenities that the public wants." I pointed out that Save Our City had delayed the park, and construction costs had increased over the past year. "Save Our City needs to take some responsibility here."

They doubled down on name-calling, describing Studer as a "slick salesman, that's all he (Studer) is."

I defended Quint. "Studer is the former president of Baptist Hospital (1995-2000) who turned around that institution. He established the foundation that led to Baptist winning the Baldridge Award. INC Magazine has honored him with a Master of Business award. Studer is one of the top 20 most influential people in healthcare. He built the Studer Group from nothing. Heck, he spoke at the U.S. Naval Academy just last week."

Save Our City Spams Blog

After I posted that Save Our City was running out of money, members began posting on all my blog posts about the maritime park that Friends of the Waterfront Park had violated Florida's campaign laws.

The alleged violations involved failing to report $40,096.97 to the Appleyard Agency in December 2005. A Studer check to the committee had been made in January 2006 to cover the payment made in December. Save Our City also claimed that Bob Hart's law firm had done in-kind legal work for the park proponents that had not been appropriately reported.

Jeff DeWeese responded:

Rick,

The issue alleged occurred in Dec / Jan, prior to city council approval or any issue or election being set. We believe no campaign violations have occurred.

Bob Hart is the attorney to the PAC, and my understanding is that campaign finance laws state that legal and accounting services are not in-kind contributions that need to be listed.

Of course, if the author believes actual campaign violations have occurred, they should report them immediately to the appropriate officials.

My personal opinion is that the saddest thing about this latest smear attack is that Save Our City can't let the public get the facts about the park project and vote on whether they want the development or not. They are trying to attack good people who are trying to make Pensacola better out of desperation because the project itself withstands any of their criticisms.

Let's vote and see.

-- Jeff DeWeese

WCOA Blog Down

WCOA had to take down Luke McCoy's blog, Pensacola Speaks Forum, after unidentified people posted comments that accused Quint Studer of murdering Adm. Jack Fetterman and Mayor Emeritus Vince Whibbs.

Fetterman Night Success

The Pensacola Pelicans hosted a tremendously successful tribute to Fetterman. Jack and Nancy's son threw out the first pitch. Between the third and fourth innings, I had the privilege of presenting Nancy with a special plaque honoring their contributions to the community.

A touching moment came when Nancy presented Quint with a Los Angeles Dodgers jersey bearing the Fetterman name—a gift originally from former Dodgers manager Tommy Lasorda to Jack. Quint announced his plans to display the jersey at the Fetterman Maritime Museum.

The event drew many local officials, including Mayor John Fogg and Council members DeSorbo, Wiggins, Jerralds, and Townsend, who attended with their families. Councilman Townsend led the traditional seventh-inning stretch rendition of "Take Me Out to the Ball Game."

WEAR TV 3 Sports Director Don Shugart handled the radio play-by-play duties, with Mayor Fogg and me joining him in the broadcast booth for color commentary. Each mention of the Community Maritime Park drew enthusiastic cheers from the crowd.

The Fort Worth Cats won the game in the late innings. When I reported on the night, I added, "FYI: The division-leading FW Cats have a downtown baseball park that is very successful."

Frustrations Mount

The Chuck & Donno ads and the blog frustrated Save Our City. My strategy was to challenge every point made in their mailers, viewpoints, letters to the editor, ads, and media interviews.

At their August 2 community meeting, they announced plans to discredit Downtown Improvement Board Executive Director Kim Kimbrough because his organization supported the park. Fairchild told the members that the League of Women Voters would challenge the referendum vote if the park won.

Jeff reported that someone in the audience said, "I'm ultimately only concerned about my neighborhood. I'm selfish; I want my neighborhood taken care of and forget downtown." The comment drew applause.

Fairchild said, "Of the ninety best cities to live in, seventy-seven don't have baseball stadiums. Pensacola's biggest needs are taking care of what we have, not trying to grow."

To Jeff's disbelief, Helene Donovan said, "I have never heard anyone with Save Our City attack anyone with CMPA personally."

That same day, Fairchild told the Arts Council of Northwest Florida board, "I cannot see any way this park would benefit the arts."

He insulted the group's artists, saying, "We all know artists are poor, and they won't be able to afford to live downtown." The Arts Council board then voted to endorse the Community Maritime Park. On the blog, I recommended that Save Our City reconsider sending Fairchild to speak to groups. He wasn't helping their cause.

In early August, Save Our City sent out a robocall. The points made were bizarre. I posted the audio on the blog (boldface) and responded (italics):

"With everybody hiding who they are…" Quint Studer, UWF Pres. Dr. John Cavanaugh and Judge Lacey Collier haven't hidden.

"Who will own the condos?" What condos?

"Who will own it?" The City of Pensacola retains ownership of all the land. That's why there is a lease.

When Donovan and Fairchild spoke to the Pensacola SubWest Rotary Club, they touted a recent CRA Request for Proposal for the property at 9th Avenue and Romana Street as a prime example of the good responses and competitive bids the city would have received if we had done an "open" and "honest" RFP for the Trillium property. Their point fell on deaf ears.

McCoy Fans Opposition

A reader emailed that Luke McCoy's comments on "Pensacola Speaks" on Friday, August 4, had upset him.

Last Friday, I caught some of Luther Eason's (Luke McCoy's) 'Pensacola Speaks' as he was pontificating on the Maritime Park news. He made a comment that really burns me, and it should also ruffle a few feathers.

He stated that Dr. John Cavanaugh was only trying to gain fame so he could add to his resume and maybe, just maybe, get a job at a REAL UNIVERSITY someday. This is coming from WCOA's "Pensacola Speaks" program.

As a matter of history, WCOA was named originally Wonderful City of Advantages when it first on the air. WCOA was a mainstay for this area in the fifties, sixties, and seventies, for being the leader in local news. I know it goes against everything that Pensacola Speaks was started for.

There are a lot of good newscasters and air personalities, as well as listeners, who would be turning over in their graves. Some are still with us, such as Gordon Towne, Dave Pavlock, and Byrne Bennete, and I hope they did not tune in to what Speaks has become.

Don Priest was our version of Walter Cronkite for three decades, and I know he would never have tolerated putting people down who are only helping keep our city moving. Foreword, I was lucky enough to have worked in the newsroom with some of them. Ironically, Wonderful City of Advantages is becoming a one-sided forum. Maybe Luke could get Mark O'Brien to team up with him.

I know society changes, and "Radio ain't what it used to be." When your paper first started, it provided a way to get information out to the readers, and your team has carried that forward. There are a lot of times that I disagree with what you write, but you at least do it fairly.

This is not a letter to the editor … just a chance to say that I, along with many other citizens, am ashamed of the slander against the UWF President. Maybe they changed the meaning of WCOA to the Wonderful City of A………

Thanks for letting me vent and, at the same time, for informing you of McCoy's rantings.

We began assigning our reporters to listen to "Pensacola Speaks." On Monday, August 7, McCoy again had Donovan as his guest. For the first time, the councilman said that he met Quint Studer and park proponents on December 28, 2004, and they begged him to support the project. He talked about losing control of the site because of the lease, positioning himself and McCoy as positive people and the Friends of the Waterfront Park as negative ones.

McCoy called the park supporters "lapdogs" and "bottom-feeders," adding that listeners may not like his opinion, but his opinion wasn't bought.

On the blog, I wrote about the irony of Donovan saying, "I believe we should talk about issues in the public."

In March, he had gotten caught privately lobbying ECUA board members to pressure the City of Pensacola for more money to relocate the Main Street Sewage Treatment Plant. Donovan wanted the public to believe the city didn't have the funds to develop the maritime park.

Save Our City's New Slogan

Our constant hammering that the park opponents had no plan for the Trillium site prompted Save Our City to change the slogan on its political flyers and yard signs to: "Vote No—We can build a better waterfront park."

I teased:

"Hmmm, so now they like the park, but they want to say what's built. That should clear things up.

Under the new slogan, you should vote 'Yes' if you want a multi-use stadium, conference center, UWF classrooms, maritime museum, shop, restaurants, entertainment, fishing pier, and waterfront park. All profits will go to local charities, the city retains control and ownership, and taxpayers outside the CRA pay nothing.

If you vote "No," what do you get?"

I joked that their new yard sign should simply say, "No trespassing."

Donovan Emails

Independent News finally obtained Councilman Donovan's emails on Friday, August 11, after nearly a month of waiting. The total cost for processing the request was $120.35, with $110 charged by the councilman for copies and clerical work, and $10.35 charged by the city.

These emails, primarily exchanges between Donovan and a small circle including Fairchild, Elebash, Donovan's wife Helene, and two regular letter writers to the daily newspaper, William Cobb and P.A. Ucci, revealed Save Our City's behind-the-scenes operations.

The correspondence showed Elebash's deeper and earlier involvement in Save Our City than previously known. He actively coached Donovan and Fairchild on their City Council meeting presentations, emphasizing key talking points: "Studer, ballpark, the $100 million project, economic impact study." Notably, Elebash advised Donovan to avoid discussing the Port of Pensacola, viewing it as a distraction from their main message.

Despite their public claims of having no grievance with Quint, the emails exposed that Elebash, Donovan, and Fairchild had deliberately planned to make him a central issue. The retired UWF professor particularly relished the prospect of challenging Studer, as evidenced in a viewpoint shared with Donovan and Fairchild that he wanted the PNJ to publish after the council vote.

In one telling email to Fairchild, Elebash wrote: "Victory this time will be sweeter than last time. In 2003, we were fighting City Hall. This time, the adversary is a very wealthy man who has already spent $600,000 promoting the project and who has intimidated the council."

When I published these emails on the blog throughout the latter half of August, they painted a clear picture: Donovan, Fairchild, and their associates had set their minds on opposing the maritime park proposal from its first council presentation in January 2005. Rather than constructively participating in the numerous public town hall meetings and workshops to improve the park's design, they undermined the entire project.

I added, "They never thought anyone would ask to see their emails, even though they had asked the city, CMPA, and UWF for theirs. They are bullies who have gotten comfortable saying anything they like without being challenged. They aren't accustomed to being held accountable."

I began to feel the momentum shifting toward the Community Maritime Park. Save Our City's tactics, which worked so well in 2003, were not resonating with voters.

Chapter 26:
The Home Stretch

August 2006

On Monday, August 14, the Pelicans announced that they were on pace to set an attendance record at Pelican Park on the UWF campus. : Even though the team had a losing record (12-23) and was twelve games out of first place in the American Association's Southern Division, the Pelicans averaged 1,655 fans per game. At noon, Mort O'Sullivan and Charlie Fairchild debated the Community Maritime Park before the Pensacola Five Flags Rotary Club.

"No real fireworks, although O'Sullivan got very passionate about the project and earned applause several times," I wrote on the blog. "Even though that particular Rotary has an older membership, the crowd wasn't as friendly to Fairchild as he had hoped. He tried all his best lines—emails show a conspiracy, $100 million giveaway, the need for a national RFP."

I continued, "However, one Rotarian told me that Fairchild just kept speaking in circles. Several members were frustrated that their new campaign signs say they can build a better park, but Fairchild offered no alternative plans or ideas. Fear and negativity don't work well on Rotarians. O'Sullivan won the debate."

Save Our City Parodies

In mid-August, we announced the formation of a new PAC to battle Save Our City's misinformation campaign.

"The Independent News staff is fed up with the disingenuous rhetoric of Save Our City PAC," I wrote on the blog. "Therefore, we're forming the Better Save Our City (BSOC) Social Club. Our mission is to enlighten the public on capital projects and community initiatives that we believe are for the betterment of Pensacola and all of Northwest Florida, and to complain about and lampoon those who we believe are holding back the area. Coronas are optional. We hope to hold a press conference soon to announce our bylaws and upcoming events. Our slogan is 'We can build a better Save Our City.'"

Jeff actually incorporated the committee. The BSOC message was: "Fun, Coronas, cookies, cute girls, hot guys, and smart as hell."

Chamber Supports Park

On Thursday, August 17, the Pensacola Chamber announced its support for the Community Maritime Park, stating it "offers an unprecedented vision for the future of Pensacola's downtown."

"Developing the waterfront will be a tremendous benefit for the city on its own, but the Community Maritime Park will act as a catalyst for further economic development that is likely to follow," stated the press release. "Not only will property values increase, but the Community Maritime Park will bring a vibrancy to the city which will give our citizens and future generations something from which to build a greater Pensacola."

The chamber pointed out that a recent study recommended three strategies for strengthening the core business community: 1) Attract and retain talent; 2) Foster innovation and industry; and 3) Enhance the quality of downtown.

The chamber said, "The Community Maritime Park accomplishes all this and more."

The organization encouraged members to support the Community Maritime Park. "Please make a commitment to picking up ten signs— one to keep and nine to distribute to your friends and associates."

The Chamber's endorsement drew the wrath of Save Our City. I received this anonymous email:

The downtown Pensacola Chamber of Commerce office is located on the south side of Garden Street in Pensacola. Their blinders seem to prevent them from looking in any direction other than South.

Taxpayers' money spent south of Garden Street can only benefit them. Spending $40,000,000+ of taxpayer money is a great idea, especially when the residents from the rest of the community have to make up for the property tax dollars looted from the City and County general fund budgets.

Based on hundreds of hours of public input meetings, we know the community has asked for public space along the water, green space in which to plan festivals and outdoor events, plus shops, restaurants, and entertainment.

But the most notable item is never mentioned. The Downtown Chamber has never done any independent study to verify anything about the project. They accept as fact the song and dance being proposed by the CMPA folks. Did you ever wonder why?

Fact: All of the members of the Community Maritime Park Associates (CMPA) are also members of the inner circle of the Downtown Chamber of Commerce. The three spokespeople of the CMPA are the current chairman, the immediate past chairman, and the next year's chairman. The major benefactor of the CMPA money and land grab is a board member; Other CMPA members hold important committee positions. The tentacles of the Chamber run everywhere, and now they want to wrap themselves around our waterfront.

If the city really wants "Green Space," then they should clear the land, plant grass and trees, construct some sidewalks and public restrooms, and leave the rest to Mother Nature. The city could build this "Green" area for a lot less than $40 million in debt, and we, the owners of the property, should not have to construct a $16,000,000 baseball stadium in order to enjoy our waterfront.

In the end, the waterfront area known as Trillium will not go anywhere until the ECUA Main Street sewer plant is moved. That is a $280,000,000 + project, and only two-thirds of the funds were found.

Vote No on the Maritime Park fiasco and tell your city council to start earning their pay instead of sleeping during the meetings.

———————————

I chose not to dissect the email because the points had been disproved multiple times. My readers knew the facts. However, I did offer a free beer to the reader who could pick out the most lies.

Big Check for Maritime Museum

On Friday, August 18, the University of West Florida announced that Ted Brown and Kathy Horton-Brown had committed $500,000 to the Vice Admiral John H. Fetterman State of Florida Maritime Museum and Research Center.

The gift honored the founder of Brown Marine Service Inc., Capt. S.J. Brown, who died in 2005. A shipping and tugboat-related exhibit would be established in the name of Capt. Brown.

"The Brown family has provided over three generations of maritime service to Pensacola," said Brown Marine president Ted Brown. "In honor of my father and support of the Maritime Museum, Kathy and I are proud to contribute to the University of West Florida and the greater Pensacola community."

UWF reported that private gifts and pledges to the museum now totaled more than $3.1 million. I shared my memories of Capt. Shirley Brown. He knew many of the towboat families from my hometown, Greenville, Mississippi, and loved to tell stories of the early towboat days on the Mississippi River.

"He was known for his breakfasts on his concrete yacht," I wrote. "If you were invited, you never knew who might be there—a Governor, U.S. Senator, presidential aide, or some other visiting dignitary. There was always plenty of scrambled eggs, bacon, sausage, and grits. There could be as many as a dozen people sitting around the huge tables discussing politics and the events of the day."

I added, "A visit to Pensacola by any worthwhile politician included breakfast with Shirley Brown. He deserves to be a part of the maritime museum."

Early Voting

On August 20, the day before early voting began, the PNJ published "A City Divided," which covered the positions of Save Our City and CMPA on the maritime park referendum.

Appleyard told the reporter, "This is about whether or not this town will move forward or whether we are going to send a message to anyone interested in growing this community we are hands off."

"Money, power and influence, that is what's holding our community back," said Councilman Donovan.

In his viewpoint, a young fifth-generation Pensacola resident, Evan Johns, attacked the value of minor league baseball to a city's quality of life. He said only thirteen of the towns on Money magazine's 2006 list of one hundred "best places to live" had minor league teams. Johns concluded that minor league teams are merely local attractions and have "very little or nothing to do with jobs and economic growth." He pushed the new mantra that Save Our City had begun to use: "We can build a better waterfront park."

On the blog, I questioned if Johns had written his viewpoint. "The viewpoint appears to be written by Stop Our City patron saint, C.C. Elebash. The phrase that really caught my eye was saying independent league teams are on the 'fringes' of professional baseball. Elebash has used it numerous times in emails and his viewpoints in the daily paper. He is fond of minimizing the Pelicans by calling it a fringe team, without any facts to prove his point."

I added, "The Best Places to Live analysis has been used by Charlie in his speeches to civic clubs the past two weeks. The opening about his family living here for five generations may be original, but the rest is just a rehash of the Elebash/Fairchild/Save Our City party line."

Evan Johns responded:

Dear Mr. Outzen,

I'm sorry to disappoint you. I wrote that viewpoint in today's News Journal (8/20). While I did consult with Charlie Fairchild, CC Elebash, and many others involved in Save Our City, I can write editorials all by myself. You may not have noticed that I have, in fact, been writing letters to the editor for the past year or so regarding the CMP. I am very passionate about the fact that we need other plans for the property, and I am proud to be working with them on this campaign.

I understand full well that you do not agree with my point of view, and that is fine, I accept that, but please realize that a great many of us who oppose it have made up our minds and not been swayed by talk on either side. I respect your opinions and your point of view, but I have to disagree.

It's really too bad about this project. I'd like to see a full, beautiful maritime museum. I have an issue with most of the rest of the project.

So, in closing, I wanted to inform you of the truth on the matter in a respectful way. Just because we disagree on most of these issues doesn't mean we need to be any different.

All the Best,

-Evan Johns

Trader Jon's Donation

On Monday, August 21, the Aylstock, Witkin & Sasser law firm announced it would donate Trader Joe's memorabilia, valued at over $2 million, to the Maritime Museum.

Trader Jon's was a famous downtown Pensacola bar frequented by Naval flight students, attorneys, journalists, and others for fifty years. World War II Army paratrooper Martin "Trader Jon" Weissman and his wife, Jackii, owned the bar until he died in 2000. New owners tried to keep it open, but the bar wasn't the same without Weissman.

The bar owner was known for wearing mismatched socks and offered a reward to any patron who caught him in a matching pair. His drink prices depended on the mood and how well he knew the customer. Weissman also exchanged drinks for pieces of Navy memorabilia, which led to the bar's signature collection. U.S. Senator John McCain often joked that he still had an outstanding tab at the bar.

Trader Joe's inspired the fictional club "TJ's" in the 1982 film *An Officer and a Gentleman*. Weissman made a cameo appearance on Bob Hope's TV special on the USS Lexington in 1986.

"Dammit, just when Stop Our City (our nickname for Save Our City) spent its hard-earned campaign funds on a mailer that says there is no maritime museum, another contribution to the maritime museum on the Community Maritime Park comes to light," I wrote. "We expect Stop Our City to issue a recall of all campaign materials."

Efforts Intensify

Early voting created a sense of urgency for both sides. On Tuesday, Aug. 22, the Downtown Improvement Board hosted a rally for the Community Maritime Park. Over 250 people filled Ferdinand Plaza. Pensacola Chamber Chairman Buzz Ritchie thanked the crowd for attending.

He defended the chamber's position in favor of the waterfront park. "We have always taken a position on issues that we believe are important for the community. We believe in this project and the vision of great leaders like Adm. Jack Fetterman and Mayor Vince Whibbs."

DIB President Dan Lozier read off a long list of CRA district businesses that favor the CMP. "The waterfront park plan will not raise anyone's taxes. The Downtown businesses are paying for this park—75 percent of all CRA revenues are collected from businesses, and we want this park."

When the rally ended, the crowd walked over to the Supervisor of Elections' office to vote.

Later in the day, retired insurance executive Skip Hunter and his wife, Martha Ann, announced a $1 million donation for an orchestra band shell at Community Maritime Park during a press conference hosted by UWF President John Cavanaugh. Fairchild criticized the timing of the Hunters' announcement, calling it "planned manipulation and orchestration" of the media.

Since Elebash had tried to compare Pensacola to Montgomery, Friends of the Waterfront Park invited Montgomery Mayor Bobby Bright to visit Pensacola. At a press conference, the mayor discussed how his city's Riverwalk Stadium had revitalized downtown. The $29.5 million project was funded entirely with public dollars and includes a multi-use stadium, where the Montgomery Biscuits play, and an amphitheater featuring an orchestra band shell.

At 6 p.m., Jeff called. The much-touted public meetings were now closed. He had been barred from attending the Save Our City weekly meeting and forced to sit in the Bayview Senior Center lobby, guarded by a member. They also kicked out the only 30-year-old in the meeting, who had been attending for four months. They called him a "snitch" and thought he was a reporter for us.

"Folks, watch out. This group is about to unleash political shenanigans this City has never seen," I posted on the blog. "If you have a 'Vote Yes' sign, protect it because it just may go missing. Expect more outrageous accusations. Bigger lies. More vile viewpoints in the PNJ.

Luke McCoy will either abandon the cause or become even more inane...probably the latter."

Save Our City Spin

On WCOA's "Pensacola Speaks," Councilman Donovan distanced himself from the closing of the meeting by stating that it was Fairchild's decision, not his. Then, he went on to say that Jeff deserved to be kicked out because he was taking notes on their meetings and reporting back to the Independent News.

"For over a year, Save Our City has attended public council meetings, listened to the deliberations, and then spoke out against the members," I wrote. "However, Save Our City doesn't want any opposition to attend their public meetings. If someone isn't white or a certain age and doesn't believe every position of the Save Our City leadership, then they can't be allowed to attend anymore."

I added, "Hypocrisy runs rampant in Save Our City. It is an elitist organization that masks itself as a populist group. You are only kidding yourself if you think Save Our City has this community's or your best interests in mind. Their thrill comes from stopping anything from happening. If they win, nothing will happen."

Save Our City Dirty Tricks

While early voting occurred, several park supporters reported that their "Vote Yes" yard signs were stolen. A reader wrote, "Some idiots swiped all of my 'Vote Yes!' yard signs last night and stole my brass address marker. It only makes me redouble my efforts to get people to support this wonderful project!"

Meanwhile, someone created a web link to attack the Community Maritime Park website. If you typed "www.fleecepensacola.com" into a browser, you would be redirected to propensacola.com.

Park Named

On Thursday, August 24, the Pensacola City Council voted to name the proposed Community Maritime Park in honor of the late mayor emeritus. By a 9-0 vote, the council approved the name "Vince Whibbs Sr. Community Maritime Park."

Mayor Fogg said, "Vince Whibbs continued to be engaged in the city long after he left office."

Donovan skipped the meeting. I commented, "Stop Our City co-founder Marty Donovan showed a complete lack of class last night by not showing up for the Pensacola City Council meeting."

Last Minute Events

The PNJ created a thirty-minute podcast featuring Charlie Fairchild and Mort O'Sullivan speaking with its reporters. Save Our City announced it had moved its weekly meetings off public property to its campaign headquarters. The African American Chamber of Commerce scheduled a meeting on the referendum for Wednesday, August 30, at Booker T. Washington High School. Friends of the Waterpark sent out a public invitation for a fish fry at the Trillium site from 11 a.m. to 5 p.m. on Saturday, September 2.

The big event scheduled was WSRE-TV's "Connecting the Community" at 7 p.m. on Thursday, August 31. Quint Studer and Mort O'Sullivan would face off against Charlie Fairchild and Marty Donovan and answer questions from the local media.

"It's an important community decision with implications stretching far into the future of Pensacola. We want to provide citizens with the facts in an organized and non-partisan format, one last time before the vote," stated Tony Ferguson, program producer. "We're going to have equal representation from park supporters and the opposition here. Our format will give local journalists from print, radio and television an opportunity to ask fair and balanced yet challenging questions to both sides."

WSRE moderator Robin Woods would host a panel of journalists from the Pensacola News Journal, the Independent News, WEAR-TV, and WUWF-FM. Whether or not the Independent News would have a reporter participating became a hot topic right up to airtime.

Save Our City on BLAB-TV

Save Our City booked two one-hour shows on BLAB-TV that aired live at 5:30 p.m. and 6:30 p.m. on Sunday, August 27.

In the first show, Charlie Fairchild and Marty Donovan defended not allowing park supporter Jeff DeWeese into the August 22 meeting. Charlie told a caller it was a private meeting and denied that their meetings were ever open to the public. However, the Independent News had received weekly emails inviting the public to the Save Our City meetings for months.

Donovan attacked DeWeese, calling him a "weasel" who should have been kicked out long ago. The councilman said he expected Studer to donate $2.25 million to the city, even if the referendum failed. Without the maritime park deal, Studer would have to build his office and relocate the Pensacola Pelicans elsewhere. Marty didn't explain why he would still use his capital for the Save Our City to spend.

The second show focused on their view that nothing could be done on the Trillium property until ECUA moved the Main St. Sewage Plant. The two shows were supposed to take callers, but park opponents

225

flooded the phone lines with what appeared to be predetermined questions.

The Widows Speak Out

Nancy Fetterman and Anna Whibbs issued a joint statement supporting the Maritime Park. They defended their husbands' vision and the positive potential of all the park's components.

The widows of Mayor Emeritus Whibbs and Adm. Fetterman wrote, "What began as a visionary endeavor initiated by our husbands is becoming a perversely stubborn and irresponsible protest by those who demean and diminish our husbands' affection for this city by inappropriately suggestive commentary, innuendo, and unjust remarks."

They implored voters: "Help us bring the Florida State Maritime Museum into the forefront as a flagship model, sharing the state's narrative history, which conveys with it an appreciation of diversity, culture, maritime studies, nautical archeology, technology, and environmental issues."

They ended their 1,100-word letter with: "Pensacola is the place where America began. Join us in telling the rest of the story. Vote YES for the Maritime Park on September 5."

Chapter 27:
Last Ditch Efforts

August 2006

Save Our City's C.C. Elebash created a new straw man to rally opposition against the park.

"Yes, there is a 'downtown crowd,'" he wrote in viewpoint. "The 'downtown crowd' is a loosely knit group of people who either work downtown or have financial interests downtown. It is not a formal organization. There is no membership roster. The informal membership varies from time to time and from issue to issue. They aim for the betterment of Pensacola. However, many reside outside the city, and they are sometimes out of step with city residents."

Elebash accused them of climbing on the park bandwagon without doing their homework. He stated, "Like the City Council, they were overwhelmed by the promoters. The Chamber of Commerce jumped on board without doing any independent analysis of the project. The Downtown Improvement Board (whose publication is called 'The Downtown Crowd') endorsed the proposal before it was even presented to the city council."

He predicted that the "downtown crowd," city officials, and the media would be discredited if the referendum defeated the baseball stadium. In his view, we all went "out on a limb" for the park.

Elebash wrote, "The voters will probably cut off the limb on September 5," adding, "The City of Pensacola is in trouble, and the people are ready for fresh leadership and a new direction."

I noted on the blog that the Save Our City emails proved Elebash, Donovan, and Fairchild had made up their minds against the project long before the final proposal was drafted. Elebash drafted a viewpoint against it months before the council's vote. I accused the retired professor of having a vendetta against Quint and city leadership, but I appreciated his suggestion of having younger council members.

I wrote, "In the end, I agree the city needs leadership, but I don't think it should be from a group of old white men who may be trying to relive past glory. We need more diversity and open-mindedness, or at least that's what my research says."

State Attorney Investigates

On August 29, Tom Garner requested that State Attorney Bill Eddins investigate whether the Pensacola City Council and Mort O'Sullivan violated Florida Sunshine Laws when the accountant met with council members over the Community Maritime Park. He suspected members of the Pensacola City Council may have received "unlawful compensation" to support the project.

Garner had some influence in the community. Four years earlier, the News Journal had profiled him as a community advocate who raised politicians' ire but achieved results. Environmentalists, such as park opponent Byron Keesler, saw him as a man of "uncompromising integrity."

Former County Commissioner Mike Whitehead saw him differently. In 2000, Garner filed a complaint with the Elections Commission regarding the political links between the commissioner and advertisers on Whitehead's BLAB-TV show. Whitehead received a formal reprimand and had to pay a $2,000 fine.

Whitehead told the daily newspaper, "It's a lot easier to tear down than to build. I've seen nothing constructive in anything he's doing. He antagonizes everybody he deals with."

The timing of Garner's request for an investigation could have been damaging to the Community Maritime Park referendum's passage, especially if the issue remained unresolved by September 5. His letter used the emails uncovered during numerous public records requests by Save Our City—the emails Fairchild gave to the media in July—as the basis for his allegations. Public statements from Councilman Donovan, who is not included in the accusations, were also quoted heavily.

According to the letter's footnotes, Donovan confirmed his quotes with Garner.

Garner targeted Mort because Donovan had said the accountant told him that all the councilmen were "on board with the project." Under Florida law, it's illegal for an individual to serve as a conduit by sharing how council members plan to vote on an issue before the full council.

Mayor Fogg held a press conference at City Hall refuting the accusation. "It is an allegation based on fantasy, a conspiracy theory that would be laughable if it were not so injurious to the fabric of our community."

The State Attorney's office opened an investigation. After interviewing Mort and the council members, Eddins dismissed the charges, saying that the eight councilmen and Mayor Fogg stated that Mort was never a go-between on the park idea.

Garner questioned the thoroughness of the state attorney's investigation. He told the PNJ he would file another complaint with the Florida Commission on Ethics.

Mort had taken heat from locals for so steadfastly supporting Quint. He recalled, "The feeling I got from some was, 'You're an old timer here. What are you doing associating with him?"

He blamed Donovan for Garner's complaint, which came a week before the vote. "It was pretty evident the timing was to put a cloud over this on Election Day because investigations can take a while."

When called to the state attorney's office, Mort recalled, "I told them the truth. No, I was not a conduit from one council member to another. I just told our story to each council member, and I said, 'Thank you.' The next day, the newspaper reported that the state attorney found no basis for a case."

PNJ Supports Park

The PNJ editorial board came out in favor of the Community Maritime Park in its Sunday, August 27, edition. "We urge Pensacola voters to stop talking and vote for action: Approve the park plan."

The board wrote that downtown Pensacola's tax dollars and economic base financed the infrastructure that helped expand the city into the suburbs and outlying commercial areas. It added, "Restoring an economically vibrant downtown will benefit everyone in the city."

The editorial pointed out that the park would be financed with taxes paid by businesses inside the CRA district. "What is there to talk about? We believe it is time to vote for the future and approve the Community Maritime Park."

Kerrigan's Endorsement

Attorney Bob Kerrigan and his law firm, Kerrigan, Estes, and Rankin, came out in favor of the park, noting that they had "no ulterior motives in the endorsement we now make of the Maritime Park."

Kerrigan was named to the News Journal's list of the top twenty movers and shakers in 2001 and was seen as a progressive voice that countered the town's more conservative leaders. He began his legal career in the public defender's office before shifting to private practice in 1975 to focus on personal injury law. Florida Gov. Lawton Chiles chose him to be part of his "Dream Team" that successfully sued the tobacco companies on behalf of the state.

The trial attorney created Helping Hands Legal Services to help residents deal with insurance companies after Hurricane Ivan and contributed to numerous charities.

Kerrigan was viewed as a trusted, independent voice in the community.

Kerrigan and his partners had read the documents on the city's website and asked probing questions regarding the feasibility of the proposed maritime park. After examining the criticisms, including the suggestion that taxes would increase if the park were built, they found them to be without merit.

"We conclude that the proposed park will be of great benefit to the city and the region," Kerrigan said in a written statement. "A level of trust is required in any endeavor of this magnitude. We place great stock in the participation of Judge Collier, President Cavanaugh, and many other outstanding citizens. We are also mindful of Adm. Fetterman and Mayor Whibbs' vision that this national museum would provide a tremendous economic boost to the community. We believe the overtures to include meaningful participation by the minority community are sincere, and we will watch to ensure those commitments are kept."

The firm once owned a piece of property in the middle of the Trillium tract that it had given to the city on the condition that the land be used in the public interest. Kerrigan said the project met that requirement.

He added, "We support the Maritime Park and urge its passage."

The WSRE Battle

On August 29, I received an email that the WSRE program concerning the referendum might be canceled.

"To help foster an impartial and informative program, WSRE invited working reporters to ask challenging but impartial, issue-oriented questions," wrote program producer Tony Ferguson. "Up until Monday of this week, two people who oppose the Community Maritime Park project, Charles Fairchild and Marty Donovan, were going to join the program. They have since declined, citing media bias as their reason."

He added, "As program producer for WSRE, while disappointed that the Save Our City parties have made this decision, I continue to make efforts to schedule a park opponent for Thursday's program. In discussions regarding the program, we never contemplated or even discussed canceling the program; only ways to still present the best possible information to voters."

An hour after I posted Ferguson's comments, Donovan agreed to participate in the televised debate with reservations. Another Save Our City member would substitute for Fairchild. My editor, Duwayne Escobedo, called Fairchild to convince him that the process would be fair. Fairchild responded that he had no problem with Duwayne, only me. My editor was "collateral damage."

The irony is that the debate was my brainchild. In July, Duwayne and I met with WSRE News Director Dick Rizzo and Ferguson to discuss the need for a public forum on the proposed waterfront park. All of us were concerned that so much misinformation was being distributed that voters weren't getting the facts on the park plan. Rizzo agreed and committed to organizing and televising the debate.

During the show, Duwayne asked Donovan how he believed Quint would profit from the park. The councilman went into a tirade against the Independent News, Rick's Blog, "Outtakes," which he called a "gossip column," and me. Donovan accused me of demonizing him and SOC, calling them "Hitler-like," and offending World War II veterans.

He said, "The Independent News is anything but independent and newsworthy."

Donovan said it was "irreprehensible" that I never called him for a quote for my articles. He added that he initially refused to participate in the debate because Duwayne was added at the "11th hour." The councilman never answered the question about how Quint would profit; the host let him off the hook and moved on to the next one.

In my "Outtakes," I admitted that Donovan had a reason to be upset:

Donovan has reasons to be angry with me. For the past six months, I've relentlessly challenged him and Save Our City (SOC) in "Outtakes," "Winners & Losers," and on the other opinion pages.

Their campaign to defeat the Vince Whibbs Sr. Community Maritime Park was so filled with misinformation and half-truths that I couldn't remain silent. If the waterfront park proposal was defeated, I want the plan to lose on its merits, not because of some sound bite that evokes fear, envy or mistrust.

I couldn't stand idle while the names of the late Vice Adm. Jack Fetterman and Mayor Emeritus Vince Whibbs were maligned, insinuating that they were part of a conspiracy to give away public land.

So, I went on the offensive. On our opinion page, we published the "Save Our City Misrepresentation of the Week," where we corrected misstatements made on their website. Eventually, Save Our City would edit the site and fix many of the inaccuracies.

Mark O'Brien covered the WSRE forum, noting it revealed the personalities of Studer and Donovan. About Studer, O'Brien wrote, "He's unaccustomed to being silenced. He kept talking despite the moderator's efforts to maintain time limits and focus the debate on specifics."

He criticized Donovan for spending "valuable TV time not discussing his objections but attacking a reporter for a weekly newspaper that roasts Donovan regularly."

O'Brien said he opposed the park for two reasons: "We should have sought more ideas, and we should have known the fate of the Main Street Sewage Treatment Plant before borrowing $40 million for the park."

The WSRE program didn't move the needle much for either side. The election would be decided by who could get their supporters to the polls.

Chapter 28:
The Vote

September 2006

On the eve of the September 5 primary, I reminded readers that we endorsed the Community Maritime Park early because we saw what similar progressive initiatives had done in Montgomery, Charleston, and Savannah. Save Our City had used fear, envy, and carefully planned sound bites to influence the vote: a dollar-a-year lease, tax increases, no public access, no maritime museum, no public input, just a baseball park, and a giveaway to Quint Studer.

I added, "There is no perfect waterfront park plan, but the Vince Whibbs, Sr., Community Maritime Park is a damn good one. Please vote 'yes.'"

Across town, Juanita Scott, a Black community advocate who worked at Pensacola Junior College, helped to organize the Election Day effort for Friends of the Waterfront Park.

"Juanita was the real MVP of the boots-on-the-ground effort," Quint recalled. "I had never been through an election, and she had helped with a few city council races. She was instrumental in getting out our votes."

237

Juanita first met Quint when he was the president of Baptist Hospital. She said, "I was part of the Ralph Bunche Society along with Dr. Percy Goodman, Gail Frazier, attorney Frank Gant, and a couple of others who met with Quint over concerns about having minority representation in their senior leadership team. Quint actually listened to us and hired Janice Crenshaw."

Quint's Covenant for the Community and its aim to actively promote and encourage minority participation in the contracting process also impressed her. "We had a conversation during one of the Pelican games, and he said, 'I really want to do something to enhance or move forward economic development in this community, specifically where more minority participation is involved.' Then, in the summer of 2006, he asked me to ensure the park's supporters got to the polls and voted."

Juanita, Lumon May, who was later elected county commissioner, and other Black leaders combated Save Our City's disinformation campaign in the Black neighborhoods. Juanita said, "People wanted to believe that when you have a project of this size, there's some ulterior motive for somebody to gain substantially and leave everybody else behind. And that just was not the case with this project."

Jeff DeWeese said Juanita helped him understand Pensacola's Black voters. "Juanita knew the African American voter better than anyone else in Pensacola. She taught me that you must give people in the African American community a reason to support something and show how it would benefit the entire community, not just the wealthy. She was very skilled at determining who had a real impact on the community and who did not."

On the eve of the election, Juanita wouldn't let any volunteers leave the campaign headquarters until everyone understood their assignments. "I remember saying, 'Okay, let's order in for pizza because we're not going anywhere until we have secured a strong plan for election day.' And we sat there until we came up with what I thought was a good strategic plan for making sure that our supporters got to the polls."

She added, "That did involve phone banks and trying to monitor who voted and who has not voted — a very typical plan for an election. You want to find out which of your voters have not gone through the polls yet. You want to make sure that you keep contacting them throughout the day, as many touches as you can, to make sure that they get out to the poll."

Jeff, Juanita, and pollster Bruce Barcelo figured they would need to get a minimum of 8,000 "yes" votes for the referendum to pass. Juanita recalled, "If we could get to that number, the chances of us being successful were pretty high. We broke it down by precinct within the city and looked at those individuals who were supporters. On Election Day, we made sure that we reached out to those supporters and got them to the polls."

Election Day

Friends of the Waterfront Park and the Pensacola Young Professionals manned all the city polling places, waving signs and making one final appeal for votes. Juanita and Jeff had poll watchers assigned to monitor who voted.

Jeff's spreadsheets came in handy. He explained, "We tracked all our votes when we walked the neighborhood. I still have the sheets. It was green if you were for it, red if you were against it, and yellow if you were undecided. And we knew who all of our green votes were in every single district. The poll watchers would periodically go in and see who had voted and who had not voted."

The poll watchers would call Juanita, who ran the campaign's call center. Jeff said, "Her team called those who hadn't voted: 'We noticed that you haven't made it to the polls yet. We're counting on you for the maritime vote.' Some people received as many as three calls."

Getting Out the Vote

At 11 a.m. on September 5, PYP president John Hosman sent an email to his membership:

"I have voted, have you? This is our time to make a difference in the community by voting yes for the Maritime Park. Your task today is to vote and let your voice be heard! Please pass this email on to everyone you know and ask them to vote! Pass it on…make and be the difference!!!"

Supervisor of Elections David Stafford reported steady crowds at the city precincts. He expected voting to pick up from 4 p.m. until the polls closed at 7 p.m. as voters headed home after work.

The Friends call center hustled to get those few remaining voters to the polls. Jeff said, "We had some people call us back and say we could stop calling them; they had made it to the polls."

Seville Quarter Victory Party

Park supporters gathered at Apple Annie's in Seville Quarter to await the election results. Two weeks earlier, Mort had called Quint to discuss a possible victory party, but his friend refused to talk about it, fearing he might jinx the referendum.

"He was very superstitious and got really upset about it," Mort recalled. "He didn't want to be overconfident and let up. He said, 'Don't talk about these things.' We realized we just had to have a party, so we made the plans, and we just didn't talk to him about it."

Quint shared, "I would have been disappointed if the project lost, but I knew I could wake up the next day knowing I just wanted to make Pensacola a better place to live."

241

When the polls closed, Quint sat nervously with Mort in the O'Sullivan Creel offices, a block away from Seville Quarter. Mort said, "He was just a basket case. He refused to get joyous or angry. We were constantly checking the election supervisor's website and constantly getting updates from Buzz Ritchie over the phone."

Quint called Juanita several times. She tracked what Ritchie saw at the Supervisor of Elections office and the results posted at the various city precincts. She recalled, "We wanted to know which precincts were in and those precincts that we didn't have results from yet. We had to know how many possible votes were out there that we don't know about."

Juanita said, "Quint would call and ask, 'Did we do it?' And I said, 'Well, wait a minute. Wait a minute, wait a minute.' Then finally, 'Yes, we got it.'"

By 7:30 p.m., it was clear that they had nothing to worry about. The "yes" side had earned 51 percent of the early vote, and the Community Maritime Park started to win narrowly in the Save Our City strongholds of Cordova Park, Scenic Heights, East Hill, and North Hill. The young vote had successfully nullified the opposition's elderly power base.

Still, Quint refused to celebrate until all but two of the city precincts had reported their results. Mort said, "Finally, I told him, 'C'mon, we got to go.'"

As they walked across Ferdinand Plaza, we got the results for the predominantly black precincts, and it was all over for Save Our City:

Mt. Zion Baptist - Yes: 493; No: 258

St. John Divine - Yes: 129; No: 68

Mt. Olive Baptist - Yes: 271; No: 130

Macedonia Baptist - Yes: 606; No: 479

When all precincts were tallied, the park won resoundingly, 10,297 to 8,140. Save Our City received 3,716 fewer votes than in 2003 when Fairchild and Donovan defeated the first Trillium plan. The Maritime Park won twenty-two out of twenty-nine precincts. Two precincts were lost by fewer than three votes combined.

Jeff recalled, "Honestly, I was shocked. I did not think it would win by that much. I thought we would be up all-night waiting for the results."

Juanita was exhausted but jubilant. "I was ecstatic, absolutely ecstatic."

Quint and Mort found over 200 supporters celebrating the victory when they walked into Seville Quarter. Many of the partygoers had walked neighborhoods for the park and had begun chanting Quint's name when they heard he was coming. However, Quint faced a problem. He said, "I had prepared remarks in case voters turned down the proposal, but I didn't have a victory speech."

Never truly lost for words, Quint told the cheering crowd, "We will never again hear people talk about visiting cities with better downtowns. From now on, people will say, 'You should go to Pensacola.'"

Mort hugged supporters. He said, "We will never be the same in the city again."

The results held special significance for architect Miller Caldwell, Jr., who worked on several of the project's elements. Miller initially assisted Adm. Fetterman in realizing his dream of establishing a maritime museum on Pensacola Bay, and later, the architect aided Studer in finding a location for a baseball park in the downtown area.

"I first worked independently with both, but as the opportunities came to fruition, as well as the size of the Trillium site, the overall concept began to take form," Miller recalled. "I was pleased to work with each of them to promote the partnership in the development of a diverse and exciting public/private community park."

He regretted that Fetterman and Whibbs hadn't lived to see the referendum's passage. Years later, he shared his emotions from that night.

He said, "I was filled with pride for my hometown, thrilled for Jack, Quint, and Vince, excited for all the community leaders, and eager to be part of the beginning of the redevelopment of downtown Pensacola."

Quint's attorney, Bob Hart, delayed a family trip to be at Seville Quarter. He had seen how the naysayers and negative thinkers had stymied progress in Pensacola for years, but the Community Maritime Park project was different.

"The effort led by Quint Studer and joined in by people from all walks of life was something the naysayers had never seen before," Hart recalled. "I will never forget the genuine sense of pride I felt for our community. I was convinced it was a pivotal moment for progress and a bright future for Pensacola."

Jim McClellan, a close friend, sent me an email:

In my opinion, IN and your blog made a tremendous difference in this race. You've gone from fighting the "man" to being "da man." This is a great night and a new day for Pensacola and Escambia County.

This is truly a time to celebrate and take a victory lap, but they should know this is also an opportunity to lead by example. The young professionals have shown they are serious, motivated, and ready to take this city to the next level. Now, they bear some responsibility for what the city will be like when it reaches that level.

As it turns out, there is an excellent role model to follow in that regard. Vince Whibbs was as gracious and good-hearted a person as there ever was. I guess that he would have been thrilled with the outcome, but I'm sure he would have urged civility and reconciliation afterward.

Fortunately, I believe most of these younger people are inclined toward graciousness anyway. Real winners typically are . . .

Over Coffee

At Waffle House, Quint, Mort, and I slumped in our booth, completely drained. Quint said that he felt like he'd gone twelve rounds with Muhammad Ali. Between sips of steaming coffee, Mort had us cracking up with behind-the-scenes stories I'd never heard before. We playfully ribbed each other as we relived the high points of the grueling two-year campaign.

When Mort reflected that he was feeling a mix of relief, exhaustion, and pure joy, I knew exactly what he meant. The journey had taken its toll on all of us, but knowing the voters had embraced our vision for the park made it all worthwhile.

"It restored my faith in our community," Mort said.

I couldn't help but chuckle. "Years from now, everyone will take credit for this park. Few will remember the details of this success."

My exhausted friends nodded knowingly.

"But I will," I added quietly.

Epilogue:

February 2025

The afternoon light streamed through the windows of Quint Studer's Maritime Place office, illuminating the panoramic view of Blue Wahoos Stadium and Pensacola Bay beyond. Twenty years had passed since the Community Maritime Park concept was first presented to the Pensacola City Council, and the landscape outside the window stood as testament to what vision, persistence, and community effort could achieve.

Through a complicated multi-city deal, Quint bought a Double-A Minor League Baseball team and renamed it the Pensacola Blue Wahoos. The team has won three Southern League championships, and Blue Wahoos Stadium is widely recognized as one of the premier minor league ballparks, winning the Southern League Ballpark of the Year three times and being named the Best Double-A Ballpark by Ballpark Digest in 2017 and 2019.

The Vice Admiral John H. Fetterman State of Florida Maritime Museum and Research Center and the University of West Florida Conference are missing from the park's landscape. Both were casualties of state budget cutbacks due to the recession. However, their loss hasn't stymied the city's resurgence.

Since the stadium opened in 2012, more than $250 million in private investment has poured into downtown Pensacola. The area surrounding the park, once filled with vacant lots and deteriorating buildings, now bustles with apartments, shops, restaurants, and hotels. Property values within the Community Redevelopment Area have tripled, generating tax revenue that funds additional improvements in downtown Pensacola.

Perhaps most significantly, Pensacola's demographics have shifted. Young professionals routinely left for opportunities in larger cities for decades before the park. However, the 2010s saw that trend reverse, with Pensacola experiencing population growth for the first time in generations.

In Quint's office, I reminisced with my two friends about how the 2006 referendum changed our city, and I couldn't help but smile at how far we've come.

Mort O'Sullivan, his voice carrying the weight of someone who had seen Pensacola through its ups and downs, shared how he realized something dramatic was needed after Hurricane Ivan. "I knew as we entered the new century that we were not in a good place. Government problems, economic problems, poverty," he told us. "And I knew somebody had to come along and reverse the community's prevailing negativity and stagnation."

The process would be painful but necessary. "I didn't know it would be us," he reflected. "But as this thing unfolded and I saw the vitriol rise in this community, I said we needed to fight it. We were at an impasse, and somebody had to win and push us forward."

Quint added, "We were dealing with a mindset that resisted change and couldn't envision something better."

Looking back, the fight over the Maritime Park became a proxy battle for Pensacola's future. Would we remain stuck in our old ways, or would we embrace the possibility of change?

"It was a combination of persuasion and overcoming opposition," Mort reflected. "Persuading the votes that you needed to do this, I think, went well. And then just overcoming the opposition became part of, I guess, the cleansing of the old way."

The fight wasn't easy. Our city had what Mort perfectly described as a "win-lose, not win-win" mentality. Quint, still relatively new to town at the time, admitted, "I was just naive. I just wanted to be helpful. Sometimes, if you know what you're getting into, you might not get into it."

The personal attacks were brutal, especially on Quint and his family. Mort reminded us, his voice softening, "Quint doesn't talk about it very much, but I don't know how I would've done in his shoes. The attacks that came when you used to be able to put comments after the daily newspaper's articles online were beyond unreasonable."

But something unexpected emerged from our fight—a new generation of leaders. Quint pointed out, "I think one of the benefits we had from what we went through is that it created younger generations of leaders. Whether it's John Hosman, Jason Crawford, Chad Henderson, D.C. Reeves, Katie White, Lumon May... You can no longer say to young people, 'Wait your turn.' Today, our young leaders don't wait for permission."

The maritime park's success also changed how the community approaches challenges. The contentious debates that once paralyzed progress have given way to a more collaborative process. Subsequent development projects—including ST Engineering's Aviation Maintenance, Overhaul and Repair campus, American Magic's Pensacola Center of Maritime Excellence, and the transformational Hollice T. Williams Park project—move forward with broad public support.

The shift in attitude has manifested itself in numerous ways beyond the park. Palafox Street, once dotted with vacant storefronts, was named one of the "Ten Great Streets in America" by the American Planning Association in 2013. The Gallery Nights that had once struggled to attract visitors now draw thousands each month.

The ECUA Main Street Sewage Treatment Plant, whose stench had plagued downtown for decades, was finally demolished in 2011. The

$316 million Central Water Reclamation Facility that replaced it won engineering awards for its innovative design.

I asked Mort and Quint if the Community Maritime Park had met their expectations.

"It exceeded mine," Mort said. "I didn't think you could build a stadium this nice for what little money was allocated to this project. And the way that the grounds have generally been kept since we've started this thing, this has become a point of beauty in our community."

Quint agreed but admitted he didn't know if the park would work. "I'd never done this. We were guessing it would go. We wanted a community gathering spot. I wanted the stadium and its concourse to be Main Street, and it's exceeded that expectation."

He continued, "We just had the Double Bridge Run at the stadium, and it seems like nearly every weekend, something is going on— different ages, different races, different causes. You come here in the morning; people walk around the park for exercise. At night, people start driving up around sunset to watch the sunset."

Quint credited former City Manager Tom Bonfield for planting the seed that brought him to downtown Pensacola.

"It all started with Tom Bonfield. He invited me to breakfast and asked about me relocating Studer Group to downtown," he shared. "It was his idea, not mine. I'm not a strategic planner; I'm an implementer.

Tom said, 'We are trying to attract major businesses. Would you think about building your office down here?' And that's when we started thinking about a ballpark and offices downtown."

I asked them about Jack Fetterman and Vince Whibbs, who both passed without seeing the park referendum passing.

Quint didn't hesitate. "If it wasn't for Jack, it might not have happened because he really was the key very early on. I remember him going to WEAR-TV and saying, 'Sometimes, you might think something is too good to be true, and this is one of those things that is as good as it seems.' He was so vital in terms of confidence, drive, and reputation."

"Vince also added significant credibility to the project when he came on board," Mort said. "We are lucky to have those superstars on our side."

"Jack was sort of bulletproof, bigger than life," Quint said. "When it started, he was going to be the main person. I was traveling for the Studer Group and stayed behind the scenes. I funded the campaign, and he was the face. And then, when he passed away, thank God, Vince would be the face. And I became the last man standing in some ways after Vince passed, but we had good support around me."

When we started discussing what we learned about ourselves from the referendum battle, Quint said, "If you lead with your values, you'll make these tough decisions, but it wasn't like we did this blindly. We did research. We went to Pittsburgh to meet with Ray Gindroz because I didn't want to throw my name or money at a park and have national experts say it was a stupid idea."

Quint was braver than he thought at the time. "Doing a project like this takes a lot of guts. If this doesn't work, you will be blamed for ruining the city instead of building the city."

Mort said, "I learned if you really believe in something, don't ever give up. I had a little more stick-to-itiveness than I might have predicted. This took a long time, and it ate up a lot of time from my practice. My partners might have grumbled a little bit, but they never said a word."

Sitting there with my friends, looking out over what we helped create, I couldn't help but think about how this project changed our city forever. As a newspaper publisher, I'd caught my share of hell during the fight, but as Mort reminded me with a smile, "You do that on a daily basis anyway."

"Yeah," I replied. "I think what happened is that people realized that I'm a lot smarter than they thought and maybe not as mean as they thought, but I am not afraid to fight."

Perhaps the most touching moment came when Quint shared what he told WEAR-TV after the vote passed. "They asked, 'Quint, what would you like to say?' And I said, 'Tell your children and grandchildren it's time to come back home.'"

And they have.